cooking **vegetarian**

cooking **vegetarian**

NICOLA GRAIMES

CONSULTANT AUTHOR

HERMES
HOUSE

For all recipes, **quantities** are given in both **metric** and **imperial** measures and, where appropriate, measures are also given in **standard cups** and **spoons**. Follow one set, but not a mixture, because they are **not interchangeable**.

Standard **spoon** and **cup** **measures** are level.
1 tsp = 5 ml, 1 tbsp = 15 ml, 1 cup = 250 ml/8 fl oz

Australian standard **tablespoons** are 20 ml. Australian readers should use 3 tsp in place of 1 tbsp for measuring small quantities of gelatine, cornflour, salt, etc.

Medium eggs are used unless otherwise stated.

First published in 1999 by Hermes House
Hermes House is an imprint of Anness Publishing Limited
Hermes House, 88–89 Blackfriars Road, London SE1 8HA.

© Anness Publishing Limited 1999

ISBN 1 84038 500 6

A CIP catalogue record for this book is available from the British Library

Publisher Joanna Lorenz
Editor Sarah Ainley
Copy editors Linda Doeser and Jenni Fleetwood
Photography Nicki Dowey, Michelle Garrett, Dave King, William Lingwood, Thomas Odulate and Sam Stowell
Design Wherefore Art?
Recipes Jacqueline Clarke, Roz Denny, Joanna Farrow, Kit Han, Nicola Graimes, Christine Ingram, Sallie Morris and Jennie Shapter
Production Controller Karina Han

Printed and bound in Singapore

10 9 8 7 6 5 4 3 2 1

cooking vegetarian

introduction

The **fabulous** range of healthy and delicious **ingredients** available today means that there are limitless possibilities for meat-free meals. **Fresh**, seasonal **vegetable** produce is not only nutritious, it supplies **colour**, flavour and texture to **recipes**. Essential staples such as bread, rice, pasta, potatoes, beans and pulses will provide **the base** from which **to build** your culinary creations.

the vegetarian kitchen

A **WELL-BALANCED** DIET WILL **ENSURE** YOU GET ALL THE **NUTRIENTS** YOU NEED TO **KEEP** YOUR **BODY** IN **GOOD WORKING ORDER**, AND THE GOLDEN RULE FOR ACHIEVING THIS IS TO EAT, IN **MODERATION**, A **WIDE VARIETY** OF **FOODS**.

RICE

As the staple ingredient in biryanis, pilaffs, fried rice dishes, sushi, risottos, paellas and jambalayas, rice is an extremely versatile food. Rich in complex carbohydrates and low in salt and fat, all rice is good for you, although brown rices, which retain the rice bran, have higher levels of dietary fibre. A huge number of rices are available, although the commercially prepared easy-cook varieties are poor substitutes for the real thing. Aromatic basmati rice is the traditional choice for curries and can be used, too, in a range of pilaffs and sweet rice desserts. Long grain rices, likewise, have any number of uses, while the delicate and slightly sticky Thai rices are particularly good for stir-fries and puddings. Any medium or short grain rice can be used to make paella, but only a risotto rice will make a risotto.

PASTA

Pasta is another good source of complex carbohydrates, and is the favourite of many a cook in a hurry. Available fresh or dried, in a multitude of colours, shapes and flavours, pasta should be cooked to a tender texture but should retain a firm bite, which the Italians call *al dente*. Cook pasta in plenty of boiling salted water according to the instructions on the packet, then drain, rinse in cold water and shake lightly (Italians serve their pasta slightly wet), then return it to the pan with some olive oil and seasoning. Wholewheat pastas have a nutty flavour and a chewy texture, and are particularly good in creamy sauces such as macaroni cheese. Choose pasta shapes to match the sauce: long thin pastas such as linguine and spaghetti are best served with light sauces; shells and tubes are complemented well by creamy or robust sauces.

POTATOES

Potatoes are beginning to enjoy something of a culinary renaissance as more cooks realize that choosing the right variety for the dish is one of the secrets of success. More potatoes are being grown for their flavour, and are often best served simply boiled in their skins and lightly dressed with olive oil or butter. Choose small, waxy potatoes for salads, larger, firmer ones for roasting, and floury varieties for mashing. More and more producers are now printing suitable uses on the bags, so check the labels before you buy.

PULSES

Pulses are an excellent source of protein. An exciting, almost endless variety of pulses is available. Dried pulses benefit from being soaked before being drained and boiled in fresh water. Do not add salt or lemon juice during cooking as this will toughen the skins, although you can add flavour with fresh herbs and onion slices. As with pasta, do not overdrain pulses but leave them slightly wet, then season and dress with extra virgin olive oil. Some lentils can be cooked without pre-soaking. Small split red lentils make great thickeners for soups and stews, while split peas and red lentils make good dips. Butter beans, kidney beans, cannellini, haricots, borlotti, pinto and flageolet beans are all perfect for soups, pâtés and purées. Chickpeas and aduki beans hold their texture well when cooked, and make a good base for burgers and stews.

CHEESE

A high protein food and very often a principal ingredient in vegetarian dishes. For a fuller flavour, choose well matured varieties of cheese, such as mature farmhouse Cheddar or fresh Parmesan – this way you will not need to use so much. Many vegetarians prefer to use cheeses made with vegetarian rennet; these are now widely available from healthfood stores and supermarkets, and many of the more popular cheeses are also now being made in this way. For cooking, choose full-flavoured cheeses: storing them unwrapped in the fridge will dry them out and help to concentrate the flavour so that they go further when grated. Lower fat cheeses do not have anything like the flavour of normal cheeses, so resist the temptation to use more of them. Low fat soft cheese and goats' cheeses are ideal for stirring into hot food to make instant, creamy sauces for pasta dishes and savoury bakes.

DAIRY PRODUCTS

Cultured dairy products offer the home cook lots of exciting possibilities. Crème fraîche is a high-fat, French-style soured cream which does not curdle when boiled, and is ideal stirred straight into hot dishes. It can also be whipped, to add a light piquancy to desserts. Fromage frais is a lighter, lower fat to virtually fat-free "cream", which is perfect for use on baked potatoes or in dressings and desserts. Quark is a soft cheese made from skimmed milk; it is traditionally used in cheesecakes, but is good for savoury dishes too. Cream and cottage cheese are old time favourites for all manner of sweet and savoury cooking purposes. Always check cheese labels to see if they have been made using vegetarian rennet.

SOYA

The soya bean is a natural source of vegetable protein, and makes an ideal base for the dairy-free milks, creams, spreads, ice creams and cheeses commonly eaten by vegans and those with dairy product allergies. Tofu, or beancurd, is made from soya milk, and is a particularly useful ingredient in vegetarian cooking. On its own, tofu has little flavour but it is ideal to use as an absorber of other flavours, which is why it is so popular in Oriental cooking. Firm tofu can be cut into cubes, marinated or smoked, and tastes good fried in oil or grilled to a crust. A softer set tofu, called silken tofu, is a good substitute for cream, and works well in all areas of cooking, from soups and stews to puddings and desserts.

HERBS

Wherever possible, use fresh herbs in cooking. There are many that grow well in pots and gardens, and fresh herbs are now easy to find in supermarkets. The most useful herbs for cooking are flat leaf parsley, coriander, dill, basil, chives and mint. Experiment with herbs, bearing in mind that more pungent herbs, such as tarragon, rosemary and sage, should be used in measured quantities. A handful of fresh herbs can be tossed into green salads, roughly chopped. Store leafy herbs loosely in plastic bags in the fridge, spraying them lightly with water if they look limp. Buy dried herbs in small amounts and store them in a cool, dry cupboard to retain their flavour.

SPICES

Warm, aromatic and colourful spices can transform a simple dish into a taste sensation. Experiment to discover which flavour combinations you like the best, adding cautious pinches at first and building up the flavour. Some spices, such as nutmeg, cinnamon, mace, cloves, cardamoms and ginger, can be used in both sweet and savoury dishes. Others, such as fenugreek, turmeric, paprika, cumin, coriander and chilli, are used for savoury dishes only. Spices are best roasted or fried first to bring out their aromatic oils: do this in a hot oven or in a frying pan. Use seeds or grains of spices, where possible, and grind them in a spice mill, or using a mortar and pestle. Saffron is best soaked in warm milk or water first to bring out its full flavour and fabulous colour.

A

B

C

A: Clockwise from top left, cereals such as semolina, buckwheat flour, millet, barley, whole rolled porridge oats and raw buckwheat (centre) supply protein to the vegetarian diet.

B: Clockwise from top, green, red and white cabbage, beetroot, courgettes, carrots, potatoes, parsnips and mushrooms. Fresh seasonal vegetables provide taste, colour and nutrition.

C: Clockwise from top left, polenta, red kidney beans, black kidney beans and haricot beans. Grains and pulses are vegetarian staples, and are used for many vegetarian dishes, including soups, stews and casseroles, pâtés, purées and dips.

soups

sweetcorn & potato chowder

THIS **CREAMY**, **CHUNKY** SOUP IS **RICH** WITH THE **SWEET TASTE** OF CORN AND IS **EXCELLENT** SERVED WITH **CRUSTY BREAD** AND **TOPPED** WITH **MELTED** CHEDDAR **CHEESE**.

method

SERVES 4

1 Put the onion, garlic, potato, celery and green pepper into a large heavy-based saucepan, together with the oil and butter.

2 Cook over a medium heat until sizzling, then reduce the heat to low. Cover and cook gently, shaking the pan occasionally, for about 10 minutes.

3 Pour in the stock or water, season with salt and pepper to taste and bring to the boil. Reduce the heat, cover again and simmer gently for about 15 minutes, until the vegetables are tender.

4 Add the milk, beans and sweetcorn – including their liquids – and the sage. Simmer, uncovered, for 5 minutes. Check the seasoning and serve hot, sprinkled with grated cheese.

cook's tip
If you prefer to use dried flageolet beans, soak them for about 4 hours in water before cooking. Discard the soaking water before cooking, then boil them briskly in unsalted water for 10 minutes, and simmer for 1–2 hours until tender.

ingredients

1 **onion**, chopped

1 **garlic** clove, crushed

1 medium **baking potato**, chopped

2 **celery** sticks, sliced

1 small **green pepper**, seeded, halved and sliced

30ml/2 tbsp **sunflower oil**

25g/1oz/2 tbsp **butter**

600ml/1 pint/2½ cups **vegetable stock** or **water**

300ml/½ pint/1¼ cups **milk**

200g/7oz can **flageolet beans**

300g/11oz can **sweetcorn kernels**

pinch of **dried sage**

salt and freshly ground **black pepper**

grated **Cheddar cheese**, to serve

USE **VERY YOUNG SPINACH** LEAVES TO PREPARE THIS **LIGHT** AND **FRESH-TASTING** SOUP.

ingredients

675g/1½lb fresh **spinach leaves**, washed

45ml/3 tbsp **extra virgin olive oil**

1 small **onion**, finely chopped

2 **garlic cloves**, finely chopped

1 small fresh **red chilli**, seeded and finely chopped

225g/8oz/generous 1 cup **risotto rice**

1.2 litres/2 pints/5 cups **vegetable stock**

salt and freshly ground **black pepper**

shavings of **Parmesan cheese**, to garnish

spinach & rice soup

method

SERVES 4

1 Place the spinach in a large saucepan with just the water that clings to its leaves after washing. Add a pinch of salt. Heat until the spinach has wilted, then remove from the heat and drain, reserving any liquid.

2 Either chop the spinach finely using a large knife or place in a food processor and process to a fairly coarse purée.

3 Heat the oil in a large saucepan. Add the onion, garlic and chilli and cook over a low heat, stirring occasionally, for 4–5 minutes, until softened. Add the rice and stir until well coated in the oil, then pour in the vegetable stock and reserved spinach liquid. Bring to the boil, lower the heat and simmer for 10 minutes.

4 Add the spinach and season to taste with salt and pepper. Cook for 5–7 minutes, until the rice is tender. Check the seasoning. Ladle the soup into heated bowls and serve immediately, topped with the shavings of Parmesan cheese.

cook's tip
Buy Parmesan or Pecorino cheese in the piece from a reputable supplier, and it will be full of flavour and easy to grate or shave with a vegetable peeler.

tomato & bean soup

A **RICH**, **CHUNKY TOMATO** SOUP, WITH **BEANS** AND **FRESH CORIANDER**. SERVE WITH **OLIVE CIABATTA**.

ingredients

900g/2lb ripe
  plum tomatoes
30ml/2 tbsp **olive oil**
275g/10oz **onions**,
  roughly chopped
2 **garlic** cloves, crushed
900ml/1½ pints/3¾ cups
  vegetable stock
30ml/2 tbsp **sun-dried**
  tomato paste
10ml/2 tsp **paprika**
15ml/1 tbsp **cornflour**
30ml/2 tbsp **water**
425g/15oz can **cannellini**
  beans, rinsed and drained
30ml/2 tbsp chopped
  fresh **coriander**
salt and freshly ground
  black pepper
olive ciabatta, to serve

method

SERVES 4

1 First, peel the tomatoes. Using a sharp knife, make a small cross in each one and place in a bowl. Pour over boiling water to cover and leave to stand for 30–60 seconds.

2 Drain the tomatoes and peel off the skins. Quarter them and then cut each piece in half again.

3 Heat the oil in a large, heavy-based saucepan. Add the onions and garlic and cook for 3 minutes, or until just beginning to soften.

4 Add the tomatoes to the pan, together with the vegetable stock, sun-dried tomato paste and paprika. Season to taste with salt and pepper. Bring to the boil, lower the heat and simmer for 10 minutes.

5 Mix the cornflour to a paste with the water. Stir the beans into the soup, together with the cornflour paste. Cook for a further 5 minutes.

6 Adjust the seasoning, if necessary, and stir in the chopped coriander just before serving with olive ciabatta.

---

cook's tip
For the best flavour, use sun-ripened tomatoes for this soup, rather than tomatoes ripened under glass, which often taste insipid.

THE **ONIONS** ARE **COOKED** VERY **SLOWLY** TO GIVE THIS SOUP ITS **RICH**, **BROWN** COLOUR AND DELICIOUS **SWEET ONION FLAVOUR**.

ingredients

30ml/2 tbsp **olive oil**

25g/1oz/2 tbsp **butter**

900g/2lb **onions**, quartered
   and sliced

2 **garlic cloves**, crushed

5ml/1 tsp **caraway seeds**

15ml/1 tbsp **light brown sugar**

15ml/1 tbsp **balsamic vinegar**

10ml/2 tsp **plain flour**

1.2 litres/2 pints/5 cups
   vegetable stock

1.5ml/¼ tsp **yeast extract**

grated rind and juice of 1 **lemon**

salt and freshly ground
   black pepper

sliced **French bread** and grated
   Emmenthal cheese, to serve

caramelized onion soup

method

SERVES 4–6

1 Heat the oil and butter in a saucepan and add the onions, garlic, caraway seeds and sugar. Cover and cook gently for 20 minutes.

2 Add the balsamic vinegar and cook, uncovered, for 10 minutes more, until softened and well browned. Stir in the flour and cook over a low heat for 1 minute.

3 Turn off the heat, gradually blend in the stock and yeast extract, and season to taste with salt and freshly ground black pepper. Bring to the boil, stirring, and simmer, uncovered, for about 5 minutes.

4 Stir in the grated lemon rind and 15ml/1 tbsp of the juice and adjust the seasoning if necessary. Serve the soup topped with slices of French bread and grated Emmenthal cheese.

cook's tip

Avoid Emmenthal cheese that has too many holes or is beginning to crack. The texture should be firm and smooth. There are many versions of this cheese made throughout the world, but none has quite the same delicate, nutty flavour as authentic Swiss Emmenthal, which can easily be identified, as the word "Switzerland" will be stamped all over the rind.

spicy peanut soup

A **THICK** AND **WARMING** VEGETABLE SOUP, FLAVOURED WITH **CHILLI** AND **PEANUTS**.

method

SERVES 4–6

1 Heat the vegetable oil in a large, heavy-based saucepan. Add the onion and garlic and cook over a medium heat, stirring occasionally, for about 3 minutes, until just beginning to soften. Lower the heat, add the chilli powder and cook, stirring constantly, for 1 minute further, taking care that it does not catch on the base of the pan.

2 Add the red peppers, carrots, potatoes and celery and stir well. Cook, stirring occasionally, for a further 4 minutes.

3 Stir in the vegetable stock, peanut butter and sweetcorn kernels until thoroughly combined. Season to taste with salt and pepper. Bring to the boil, cover and simmer for about 20 minutes, or until all the vegetables are tender. If necessary, adjust the seasoning before serving, sprinkled with the chopped peanuts.

cook's tip

For a more authentic South-east Asian flavour, use sweet chilli sauce instead of chilli powder. The "hotness" of this varies considerably from brand to brand, so add it with caution to begin with. You can always stir a little extra into the soup towards the end of the cooking time.

ingredients

30ml/2 tbsp **vegetable oil**
1 large **onion**, finely chopped
2 **garlic cloves**, crushed
5ml/1 tsp **mild chilli powder**
2 **red peppers**, seeded and
  finely chopped
225g/8oz **carrots**, finely chopped
225g/8oz **potatoes**,
  finely chopped
3 **celery** sticks, sliced
900ml/1½ pints/3¾ cups
  vegetable stock
90ml/6 tbsp **crunchy
  peanut butter**
115g/4oz/⅔ cup
  sweetcorn kernels
salt and freshly ground
  black pepper
roughly chopped **unsalted
  roasted peanuts**, to garnish

italian pea & basil soup

PLENTY OF **CRUSTY COUNTRY BREAD** IS A **MUST** WITH THIS **FRESH-TASTING** SOUP.

ingredients

75ml/5 tbsp **olive oil**

2 large **onions**, chopped

1 **celery stick**, chopped

1 **carrot**, chopped

1 **garlic clove**, finely chopped

400g/14oz/3½ cups frozen **petit pois**

900ml/1½ pints/3¾ cups **vegetable stock**

25g/1oz/1 cup fresh **basil leaves**, roughly torn, plus extra to garnish

salt and freshly ground **black pepper**

freshly grated **Parmesan cheese**, to serve

method

SERVES 4

1 Heat the oil in a large saucepan and add the onions, celery, carrot and garlic. Cover the pan and cook over a low heat for 45 minutes or until the vegetables are soft. Stir occasionally to prevent the vegetables sticking to the base of the pan.

2 Add the peas and stock to the pan and bring to the boil. Reduce the heat, add the basil and seasoning, then simmer for 10 minutes.

3 Spoon the soup into a food processor or blender (or use a hand blender) and process for a few minutes until the soup is smooth. Transfer to warmed serving bowls, sprinkle with grated Parmesan and garnish with torn basil leaves.

> ### variation
> Mint or a mixture of fresh herbs, such as parsley, mint and chives could be used in place of the basil.

red lentil & coconut soup

HOT, **SPICY** AND RICHLY **FLAVOURED**, THIS **SUBSTANTIAL SOUP** IS ALMOST A **MEAL IN ITSELF**. IF YOU ARE **REALLY HUNGRY**, SERVE WITH CHUNKS OF **WARMED NAAN BREAD** OR THICK SLICES OF ANY **TOASTED RUSTIC BREAD**.

ingredients

30ml/2 tbsp **sunflower oil**

2 **red onions**, finely chopped

1 **chilli**, seeded and finely sliced

2 **garlic cloves**, chopped

2.5cm/1in piece fresh **lemon grass**, peeled and sliced

200g/7oz/1 cup **red lentils**, rinsed

5ml/1 tsp **ground coriander**

5ml/1 tsp **paprika**

400ml/14fl oz/1⅔ cups **coconut milk**

900ml/1½ pints/3¾ cups **water**

juice of 1 **lime**

3 **spring onions**, chopped

20g/¾oz/scant 1 cup fresh **coriander**, finely chopped

salt and freshly ground **black pepper**

method

SERVES 4

1 Heat the oil in a large, deep frying pan. Add the onions, chilli, garlic and lemon grass and cook, stirring occasionally, for 5 minutes, or until the onions have softened.

2 Add the lentils, ground coriander and paprika. Pour in the coconut milk and water and stir well to mix. Bring to the boil, stir, then reduce the heat and simmer for 40–45 minutes, or until the lentils are soft and tender.

3 Pour in the lime juice and add the spring onions and fresh coriander, reserving a little of each for the garnish. Season the soup to taste, then ladle into warm bowls. Garnish with the reserved spring onions and fresh coriander and serve immediately.

> ### cook's tip
> Coconut milk is available in cans, compressed blocks or powder form from Chinese and Indian foodstores and larger supermarkets. It is not the same as the "milk" from a raw coconut, but is an unsweetened liquid made from grated coconut flesh and water. It is an essential ingredient in many South-east Asian recipes, and there is not really an adequate substitute.

hot-&-sour soup

THIS **LIGHT** AND **INVIGORATING** SOUP ORIGINATES FROM **THAILAND**. IT IS BEST SERVED AT THE **BEGINNING** OF A **THAI MEAL** TO **STIMULATE** THE **APPETITE**.

method

SERVES 4

1 To make carrot flowers, cut each carrot in half crossways, then, using a sharp knife, cut four v-shaped channels lengthways. Slice the carrots into thin rounds and set aside. If time is short, just slice the carrots into thin rounds.

2 Pour the stock into a large saucepan. Reserve 2.5ml/½ tsp of the chillies and add the remainder to the pan, together with the lemon grass, lime leaves, garlic and half the spring onions. Bring to the boil, then reduce the heat and simmer for 20 minutes. Strain the stock and discard the flavourings.

3 Return the stock to the pan, add the reserved chillies, the remaining spring onions, the sugar, lime juice, coriander and salt to taste.

4 Simmer for 5 minutes, then add the carrot flowers and tofu and cook for a further 2 minutes, until the carrots are just tender. Serve hot.

cook's tip
Kaffir lime leaves have a distinctive citrus flavour. The fresh leaves can be bought from Asian shops, and some supermarkets now sell them dried.

ingredients

2 **carrots**

900ml/1½ pints/3¾ cups **vegetable stock**

2 **Thai chillies**, seeded and finely sliced

2 **lemon grass** stalks, outer leaves removed and each stalk cut into 3 pieces

4 **kaffir lime leaves**

2 **garlic cloves**, finely chopped

4 **spring onions**, finely sliced

5ml/1 tsp **sugar**

juice of 1 **lime**

45ml/3 tbsp chopped fresh **coriander**

salt

130g/4½oz/1 cup **Japanese tofu**, sliced

ingredients

50ml/2fl oz/¼ cup **olive oil**

1 small **butternut squash**,
   peeled, seeded and cubed

2 **carrots**, cut into thick rounds

1 large **parsnip**, cubed

1 small **swede**, cubed

2 **leeks**, thickly sliced

1 **onion**, quartered

3 **bay leaves**

4 **thyme** sprigs, plus extra
   to garnish

3 **rosemary** sprigs

1.2 litres/2 pints/5 cups
   vegetable stock

salt and freshly ground
   black pepper

soured cream, to serve

roasted root vegetable soup

ROASTING THE **VEGETABLES** GIVES THIS WINTER SOUP A **WONDERFUL DEPTH** OF **FLAVOUR**. YOU CAN USE OTHER **VEGETABLES**, IF YOU WISH, **DEPENDING ON** WHATEVER IS **IN SEASON**, OR WHAT YOU **HAVE IN**, BUT IT IS **IMPORTANT** THAT THEY ARE **FRESH**.

method   SERVES 6

1 Preheat the oven to 200°C/400°F/Gas 6. Put the olive oil into a large
   bowl. Add the prepared vegetables and toss until coated in the oil.

2 Place the vegetables in a single layer on 2 baking sheets. Tuck the
   bay leaves, thyme and rosemary into the vegetables.

3 Roast for 50 minutes until tender, turning the vegetables occasionally
   to make sure they brown evenly all over. Remove from the oven,
   discard the herbs and transfer the vegetables to a large saucepan.

4 Pour the stock into the pan and bring to the boil. Reduce the heat,
   season to taste, then simmer for 10 minutes. Transfer the soup to a
   food processor or blender (or use a hand blender) and process for a
   few minutes until thick and smooth.

5 Return the soup to the pan to heat through. Season and serve with a
   swirl of soured cream. Garnish each serving with a sprig of thyme.

---

cook's tip
Dried herbs can be used in place of fresh: use 2.5ml/½ tsp of each type and
sprinkle over the vegetables in step 2.

chilled almond soup

THIS SOUP COMES FROM **SOUTHERN SPAIN**, AND IS VERY **REFRESHING** TO EAT ON A **HOT DAY**. IT IS A **TYPICAL EXAMPLE** OF A SPANISH **COLD SOUP**, COMBINING JUST A **FEW** INGREDIENTS IN A **SIMPLE RECIPE**.

method

SERVES 4

1 Break the bread into a bowl and pour over 150ml/¼ pint/⅔ cup cold water. Leave for 5 minutes.

2 Put the almonds and garlic in a blender or food processor and process until very finely ground. Blend in the soaked white bread.

3 Gradually add the oil until the mixture forms a smooth paste. Add the sherry vinegar, then 600ml/1 pint/2½ cups cold water and process until smooth.

4 Transfer to a bowl and season with salt and pepper, adding a little more water if the soup is very thick. Chill for at least 2–3 hours.

5 Ladle the soup into serving bowls and scatter with the toasted almonds and skinned grapes.

cook's tip
The blanched almonds in this recipe need to be very finely ground if the texture of the soup is to be completely smooth. Unless you want to spend time pounding the almonds by hand, a food processor really is essential.

ingredients

115g/4oz fresh **white bread**, about 4 thick slices
115g/4oz/1 cup **blanched almonds**
2 **garlic cloves**, sliced
75ml/5 tbsp **olive oil**
25ml/1½ tbsp **sherry vinegar**
salt and freshly ground **black pepper**
toasted flaked almonds and **seedless green** and **black grapes**, halved and skinned, to garnish

ingredients

900g/2lb ripe **tomatoes**

1 **cucumber**

2 **red peppers**, seeded and
roughly chopped

2 **garlic cloves**, crushed

175g/6oz/3 cups fresh
white breadcrumbs

30ml/2 tbsp **white
wine vinegar**

30ml/2 tbsp **sun-dried
tomato paste**

90ml/6 tbsp **olive oil**

salt and freshly ground
black pepper

To serve

1 slice **white bread**, crust
removed and cut into cubes

30ml/2 tbsp **olive oil**

6–12 **ice cubes**

small bowl of mixed chopped
garnishes, such as **tomato**,
cucumber, **red onion**,
hard-boiled egg and
flat leaf parsley or
tarragon leaves

gazpacho

THERE ARE MANY **VERSIONS** OF THIS
REFRESHINGLY CHILLED, **PUNGENT** SOUP
FROM **SOUTHERN SPAIN**. ALL CONTAIN AN
INTENSE BLEND OF TOMATOES, PEPPERS,
CUCUMBER AND GARLIC; **PERFECT** FOR A
HOT SUMMER'S EVENING.

method

SERVES 6

1 Plunge the tomatoes into boiling water for 30 seconds, then refresh in
cold water. Peel away the skins and quarter. Peel and roughly chop the
cucumber. Mix the tomatoes and cucumber in a bowl with the
peppers, garlic, breadcrumbs, vinegar, tomato paste and olive oil and
season lightly with salt and pepper.

2 Process half the mixture in a blender or food processor until fairly
smooth. Process the remaining mixture and mix with the first.

3 Check the seasoning and add a little cold water if the soup is too
thick. Chill for several hours.

4 To finish, fry the bread in the oil until golden. Spoon the soup into
bowls, adding one or two ice cubes to each. Serve accompanied by
the croûtons and garnishes.

cook's tip
The sun-dried tomato paste has been added to accentuate the flavour of the
tomatoes. You might not need this if you use a really flavoursome variety of
sun-ripened, fresh tomatoes.

starters & savouries

potato wedges with chilli dip

FOR A **HEALTHY SNACK** WITH SUPERB **FLAVOUR**, TRY THESE **DRY-ROASTED** POTATO WEDGES. THE **CRISP SPICE** CRUST MAKES THEM **IRRESISTIBLE**, ESPECIALLY WHEN **SERVED** WITH A **CHILLI DIP**.

method

SERVES 4

1 Preheat the oven to 200°C/400°F/Gas 6. Cut the potatoes in half, then cut into eight wedges.

2 Place the wedges in a saucepan of cold water. Bring to the boil, then lower the heat and simmer gently for 10 minutes, or until the potatoes have softened slightly. Drain well and pat dry on kitchen paper.

3 Mix the oil, garlic, allspice, coriander and paprika in a roasting tin. Add salt and pepper to taste. Add the potatoes to the pan and shake to coat them thoroughly. Roast, turning the potato wedges occasionally, for 20 minutes, or until they are browned, crisp and fully cooked.

4 Meanwhile, make the chilli dip. Heat the oil in a saucepan. Add the onion and garlic and cook, stirring occasionally, for 5–10 minutes, until the onion is soft. Add the tomatoes, with their juice. Stir in the chilli and vinegar. Cook over a low heat for 10 minutes, until the mixture has reduced and thickened, then check the seasoning. Stir in the fresh coriander and serve hot with the potato wedges, sprinkled with salt and garnished with fresh coriander.

ingredients

2 **baking potatoes**, about 225g/8oz each
30ml/2 tbsp **olive oil**
2 **garlic cloves**, crushed
5ml/1 tsp **ground allspice**
5ml/1 tsp **ground coriander**
15ml/1 tbsp **paprika**
salt and freshly ground **black pepper**

For the chilli dip
15ml/1 tbsp **olive oil**
1 small **onion**, finely chopped
1 **garlic clove**, crushed
200g/7oz canned chopped **tomatoes**
1 fresh **red chilli**, seeded and finely chopped
15ml/1 tbsp **balsamic vinegar**
15ml/1 tbsp chopped fresh **coriander**, plus extra to garnish

cook's tip
To save time, parboil the potatoes and toss them with the spices in advance. Make sure the potato wedges are perfectly dry and completely covered in the mixture before you roast them.

TASTY **RICE BALLS ROLLED** IN CHOPPED **PEANUTS** AND **DEEP FRIED** MAKE A **DELICIOUS SNACK**. SERVE THEM AS THEY ARE, OR WITH **EXTRA SOY SAUCE** FOR **DIPPING**.

ingredients

1 **garlic clove**, crushed

1cm/½in piece of fresh **root ginger**, finely chopped

1.5ml/¼ tsp **ground turmeric**

5ml/1 tsp **sugar**

2.5ml/½ tsp **salt**

5ml/1 tsp **chilli sauce**

10ml/2 tsp **vegetarian fish sauce** or **soy sauce**

30ml/2 tbsp chopped **fresh coriander**

juice of ½ **lime**

225g/8oz/1⅓ cups cooked **white long grain rice**

115g/4oz **peanuts**, chopped

oil, for deep frying

lime wedges and **chilli dipping sauce**, to serve

spicy peanut balls

method

MAKES 16

1 Put the garlic, root ginger and ground turmeric in a food processor and process until the mixture forms a paste. Add the sugar, salt, chilli sauce and vegetarian fish sauce or soy sauce, together with the chopped fresh coriander and lime juice. Process briefly until thoroughly mixed.

2 Add three-quarters of the cooked rice and process until smooth and sticky. Scrape into a mixing bowl and stir in the remainder of the rice. Wet your hands and shape the mixture into thumb-size balls.

3 Roll the balls in chopped peanuts to coat evenly. Then set aside until ready to cook and serve.

4 Heat the oil in a deep fryer or wok. Deep fry the peanut balls until crisp and golden. Drain on kitchen paper and then pile on to a platter. Serve hot with lime wedges and chilli dipping sauce.

ingredients

24–28 fresh young **vine leaves**

30ml/2 tbsp **olive oil**

1 large **onion**, finely chopped

1 **garlic clove**, crushed

225g/8oz/1⅓ cups cooked **long
    grain rice**, or **mixed white**
    and **wild rice**

about 45ml/3 tbsp **pine nuts**

15ml/1 tbsp **flaked almonds**

40g/1½oz/¼ cup **sultanas**

15ml/1 tbsp snipped fresh **chives**

15ml/1 tbsp finely chopped
    fresh **mint**

juice of ½ **lemon**

150ml/¼ pint/⅔ cup
    white wine

hot **vegetable stock**

salt and freshly ground
    black pepper

fresh **mint**, to garnish

pitta bread and **garlic yogurt**,
    to serve

dolmades

NOW **POPULAR** THE **WORLD OVER**, THESE
STUFFED VINE LEAVES ORIGINATED IN
GREECE. IF YOU CAN'T LOCATE **FRESH** VINE
LEAVES, USE A PACKET OR CAN OF **BRINED
LEAVES**. SOAK THE LEAVES IN **HOT WATER**
FOR 20 MINUTES, THEN **RINSE** AND **DRY
WELL** ON KITCHEN PAPER **BEFORE USE**.

method

SERVES 4

1 Bring a large saucepan of water to the boil. Add the fresh vine leaves
and cook for about 2–3 minutes. They will darken and go limp after
about 1 minute, and simmering for 1 further minute will ensure that
they are pliable enough to use. If you are using leaves from a packet
or can, place them in a large bowl, cover with boiling water and leave
for up to 20 minutes until the leaves can be easily separated, or follow
the instructions on the packet. Rinse them under cold water and drain
well on kitchen paper.

2 Heat the oil in a small frying pan. Add the onion and garlic and fry
over a low heat for 3–4 minutes, until soft. Spoon the mixture into
a bowl and tip in the cooked rice.

3 Stir in 30ml/2 tbsp of the pine nuts and all of the almonds, sultanas,
chives and mint into the bowl with the rice. Stir in the lemon juice and
season with salt and pepper to taste. Mix well.

4 Set aside four large vine leaves. Lay a vine leaf on a clean work
surface, veined side uppermost. Place a spoonful of the filling near the
stem, fold the lower part of the vine leaf over it and roll up, folding in
the sides as you go. Stuff the rest of the vine leaves in the same way.

5 Line the base of a deep frying pan with the reserved vine leaves. Place
the dolmades close together in the pan, seam side down, in a single
layer. Pour over the wine and enough stock to just cover. Anchor the
dolmades by placing a plate on top of them, then cover the pan and
simmer gently for 30 minutes.

6 Transfer the dolmades to a plate. Cool, chill in the fridge, then garnish
with the remaining pine nuts and the fresh mint. Serve with pitta bread
and a little garlic yogurt.

cannellini bean & rosemary bruschetta

MORE **BRUNCH** THAN **BREAKFAST**, THIS DISH IS A **SOPHISTICATED** VERSION OF **BEANS ON TOAST**.

method

SERVES 4

1 Place the beans in a large bowl and cover with water. Leave to soak overnight. Drain and rinse the beans, then place in a saucepan and cover with fresh water. Bring to the boil and boil rapidly for 10 minutes. Reduce the heat and simmer for 50–60 minutes, or until tender. Drain and set aside.

2 Meanwhile, make a small cross in each of the tomatoes and place them in a bowl. Pour over boiling water to cover, leave to stand for 30 seconds, then drain, peel the skins and chop the flesh. Heat the oil in a frying pan, add the fresh and sun-dried tomatoes, garlic and rosemary. Cook for 2 minutes, until the tomatoes begin to soften.

3 Add the tomato mixture to the cannellini beans, season to taste with salt and pepper and mix well.

4 Rub the bread slices with the cut sides of the garlic clove, then toast lightly. Spoon the cannellini bean mixture on top of the toast. Sprinkle with basil leaves and drizzle with a little extra olive oil before serving.

cook's tip

Canned cannellini beans can be used instead of dried. Use 275g/10oz/2 cups drained, canned beans and add to the tomato mixture in step 3. If the beans are canned in brine, then rinse and drain them well before use.

ingredients

150g/5oz/⅔ cup **dried cannellini beans**

5 **tomatoes**

45ml/3 tbsp **olive oil**, plus extra for drizzling

2 **sun-dried tomatoes** in oil, drained and finely chopped

1 **garlic clove**, crushed

30ml/2 tbsp chopped fresh **rosemary**

salt and freshly ground **black pepper**

a handful of fresh **basil leaves**, to garnish

To serve

12 slices Italian-style **bread**, such as **ciabatta**

1 large **garlic clove**, halved

grilled aubergine parcels

THESE ARE **DELICIOUS** LITTLE **ITALIAN BUNDLES** OF **TOMATOES**, **MOZZARELLA** CHEESE AND **BASIL**, **WRAPPED** IN SLICES OF **AUBERGINE** AND GRILLED UNTIL **GOLDEN**.

ingredients

2 large, long **aubergines**
225g/8oz **mozzarella cheese**
2 **plum tomatoes**
16 large **basil leaves**
salt and freshly ground
   black pepper
30ml/2 tbsp **olive oil**

For the dressing
60ml/4 tbsp **olive oil**
5ml/1 tsp **balsamic vinegar**
15ml/1 tbsp **sun-dried**
   tomato paste
15ml/1 tbsp **lemon juice**

For the garnish
30ml/2 tbsp toasted **pine nuts**
torn **basil leaves**

method

SERVES 4

1 Remove the stalks from the aubergines and cut the aubergines lengthways into thin slices – the aim is to get 16 slices in total, disregarding the first and last slices (each about 5mm/¼in thick). (If you have a mandolin, it will cut perfect, even slices for you; otherwise, use a long-bladed, sharp knife.)

2 Bring a large pan of salted water to the boil and cook the aubergine slices for about 2 minutes, until just softened. Drain the sliced aubergines, then dry on kitchen paper.

3 Cut the mozzarella cheese into eight slices. Cut each tomato into eight slices, not counting the first and last slices.

4 Take two aubergine slices and place on a flameproof tray or dish, arranged in a cross. Place a slice of tomato in the centre, season with salt and pepper, then add a basil leaf, followed by a slice of mozzarella, another basil leaf, a slice of tomato and more seasoning.

5 Fold the ends of the aubergine slices around the mozzarella and tomato filling to make a neat parcel. Repeat with the rest of the assembled ingredients to make eight parcels. Chill the parcels in the fridge for about 20 minutes.

6 Meanwhile, make the tomato dressing. Whisk together the olive oil, vinegar, sun-dried tomato paste and lemon juice. Season to taste with salt and pepper.

7 Preheat the grill. Brush the aubergine parcels with olive oil and cook for about 5 minutes on each side, until golden. Serve hot, drizzled with the dressing and sprinkled with pine nuts and basil.

polpettes

DELICIOUS LITTLE **FRIED MORSELS** OF
POTATO AND **GREEK FETA** CHEESE,
FLAVOURED WITH **DILL** AND **LEMON JUICE**,
THESE MAKE A **WONDERFUL** STARTER OR A
SCRUMPTIOUS SNACK AT ANY TIME OF DAY.

method

SERVES 4

1 Boil the potatoes in their skins in lightly salted water until soft. Drain, then peel while still warm. Place in a bowl and mash. Crumble the feta cheese into the potatoes and add the spring onions, dill, egg and lemon juice and season to taste with salt and pepper. (Feta is salty, so taste before you add salt.) Stir well.

2 Cover the mixture and chill until firm. Divide the mixture into walnut-size balls, then flatten them slightly. Dredge with flour. Heat the oil in a frying pan and fry the polpettes until golden brown on each side. Drain on kitchen paper and serve at once.

ingredients

500g/1¼lb **potatoes**

115g/4oz **feta cheese**

4 **spring onions**, chopped

45ml/3 tbsp chopped fresh **dill**

1 **egg**, beaten

15ml/1 tbsp **lemon juice**

salt and freshly ground
   black pepper

flour, for dredging

45ml/3 tbsp **olive oil**

cook's tip

Feta was originally made from ewe's milk, but nowadays it is more frequently made from cow's milk. It is white and firm, with a crumbly texture and has a fairly bland, slightly salty flavour. In Greece, where it originated, it is usually sold young in the brine bath in which it has been preserved. Elsewhere, it is more commonly available in vacuum packs. A vegetarian version is available.

ingredients

2 x 425g/15oz cans **chick-peas**

2 **garlic cloves**, crushed

1 bunch **spring onions** (white

    parts only), chopped

10ml/2 tsp **ground cumin**

10ml/2 tsp **ground coriander**

1 fresh **green chilli**, seeded and

    finely chopped

30ml/2 tbsp chopped

    fresh **coriander**

1 small **egg**, beaten

30ml/2 tbsp **plain flour**

seasoned flour, for shaping

oil, for shallow frying

salt and freshly ground

    black pepper

lemon wedges and fresh

    coriander, to garnish

For the tahini and lemon dip

30ml/2 tbsp **tahini**

juice of 1 **lemon**

2 **garlic cloves**, crushed

chick-pea & coriander cakes

THESE **SPICY** LITTLE **CAKES** ARE EQUALLY **GOOD** SERVED **HOT** OR **COLD**. FOR A MORE **SUBSTANTIAL SNACK**, **TUCK** THEM INTO POCKETS OF **PITTA BREAD** WITH SALAD.

method

SERVES 4

1 Drain the chick-peas thoroughly. Tip them into a blender or food processor and process until smooth. Add the garlic, spring onions, cumin and ground coriander. Process again until well mixed.

2 Scrape the mixture into a bowl and stir in the chilli, fresh coriander, egg and flour. Mix well and season to taste with salt and pepper. If the mixture is very soft, add a little more flour. Chill for about 30 minutes to firm the mixture.

3 Make the dip. Mix the tahini, lemon juice and garlic in a bowl, adding a little water if the sauce is too thick. Set aside.

4 Using floured hands, shape the chick-pea mixture into 12 cakes. Heat the oil in a frying pan and fry the cakes, in batches, for about 1 minute on each side, until crisp and golden. Drain on kitchen paper and serve with the dip and lemon and coriander garnish.

variation

Another quick and easy sauce is made by mixing Greek-style yogurt with a little chopped chilli and fresh mint.

vegetable spring rolls

CRISPY **SPRING ROLLS**, SERVED WITH A **SWEET CHILLI DIPPING SAUCE**, CAN BE ENJOYED AS A **STARTER**, AS PART OF A COMPLETE **CHINESE MEAL**, OR AS A **DELICIOUS** LATE **EVENING SNACK**.

ingredients

25g/1oz **rice vermicelli noodles**
groundnut oil, for stir-frying
5ml/1 tsp grated fresh **root ginger**
2 **spring onions**, finely shredded
50g/2oz **carrot**, finely shredded
50g/2oz **mangetouts**, shredded
25g/1oz young **spinach** leaves
50g/2oz fresh **beansprouts**
15ml/1 tbsp chopped fresh **mint**
15ml/1 tbsp chopped fresh **coriander**
30ml/2 tbsp **Thai fish sauce** (**nam pla**)
20–24 **spring roll wrappers** each 13cm/5in square
1 **egg white**, lightly beaten
vegetable oil, for deep frying

For the dipping sauce
50g/2oz/4 tbsp **caster sugar**
50ml/2fl oz/¼ cup **rice vinegar**
2 fresh **red chillies**, seeded and finely chopped

method

SERVES 4

1 First make the dipping sauce: place the sugar and vinegar in a small pan with 30ml/2 tbsp water. Heat gently, stirring until the sugar dissolves, then boil rapidly until it forms a light syrup. Stir in the chillies and leave to cool.

2 Soak the noodles according to the packet instructions, then rinse and drain well. Using scissors, snip the noodles into short lengths.

3 Heat a wok until hot. Add 15ml/1 tbsp oil and swirl it around. Add the ginger and spring onions and stir-fry for 15 seconds. Add the carrot and mangetouts and stir-fry for 2–3 minutes. Add the spinach, beansprouts, mint, coriander, fish sauce and noodles and stir-fry for a further minute. Set aside to cool.

4 Take one spring roll wrapper and arrange it so that it faces you in a diamond shape. Place a spoonful of filling just below the centre, then fold up the bottom point over the filling.

5 Fold in each side, then roll up tightly. Brush the end with beaten egg white to seal. Repeat until all the filling has been used.

6 Half-fill a wok with oil and heat to 180°C/350°F or until a cube of bread browns in 30 seconds. Deep fry the spring rolls, in batches, for 3–4 minutes, until golden and crisp. Drain on kitchen paper. Serve hot with the sweet chilli dipping sauce.

lunches & suppers

potato cakes with goat's cheese

GRILLED GOAT'S CHEESE MAKES A
DELICATELY **TANGY** AND **GENTLY BUBBLING**
TOPPING FOR THESE **HERBY POTATO** CAKES.
SERVE WITH A **FLAVOURSOME SALAD**.

method

SERVES 2–4

1 Coarsely grate the potatoes. Using your hands, squeeze out as much
   of the thick starchy liquid as possible, then gently combine with the
   chopped thyme, garlic, spring onions and seasoning.

2 Heat half the oil and butter in a non-stick frying pan. Add 2 large
   spoonfuls of the potato mixture, spacing them well apart, and press
   firmly down with a spatula. Cook for about 3–4 minutes on each side
   until golden.

3 Drain the potato cakes thoroughly on kitchen paper and keep warm in
   a low oven. Heat the remaining oil and butter in the frying pan and fry
   2 more potato cakes in the same way with the remaining mixture.
   Meanwhile preheat the grill.

4 Cut the cheese in half horizontally and place one half, cut side up, on
   each potato cake. Grill for 2–3 minutes, until lightly golden. Serve on
   plates and arrange the dressed salad leaves around them. Garnish with
   fresh thyme sprigs.

ingredients

450g/1lb floury **potatoes**
10ml/2 tsp chopped fresh **thyme**
1 **garlic clove**, crushed
2 **spring onions** (including the
   green parts), finely chopped
30ml/2 tbsp **olive oil**
50g/2oz/4 tbsp **unsalted butter**
2 x 65g/2½oz firm
   goat's cheese
salt and freshly ground
   black pepper
thyme sprigs, to garnish
salad leaves, such as **curly
   endive**, **radicchio** and
   lamb's lettuce, tossed in
   walnut dressing, to serve

cook's tip
These potato cakes make great party
snacks. Make them half the size and
serve warm on a large platter.

ingredients

butter, for greasing

1 litre/1¾ pints/4 cups **water**

5ml/1 tsp **salt**

250g/9oz/2¼ cups quick-
cook **polenta**

5ml/1 tsp **paprika**

2.5ml/½ tsp **ground nutmeg**

30ml/2 tbsp **olive oil**

1 large **onion**, finely chopped

2 **garlic cloves**, crushed

2 x 400g/14oz cans
chopped **tomatoes**

15ml/1 tbsp **tomato purée**

5ml/1 tsp **sugar**

salt and freshly ground
black pepper

75g/3oz/¾ cup grated
Gruyère cheese

baked cheese polenta with tomato sauce

POLENTA, OR CORNMEAL, IS A **STAPLE FOOD** IN **NORTHERN ITALY**. IT IS COOKED LIKE A SORT OF **PORRIDGE**, AND **EATEN SOFT**, OR **ALLOWED TO COOL** AND SET, CUT INTO **SHAPES**, THEN **BAKED** OR **GRILLED**.

method

MAKES 16

1 Line a rectangular baking tin or Swiss roll tin (about 28 x 18cm/ 11 x 7in) with clear film. Grease a large ovenproof dish.

2 Bring the water to the boil with the salt in a large saucepan. Pour in the polenta in a steady stream and cook, stirring constantly, for 5 minutes. Beat in the paprika and ground nutmeg, then pour into the prepared tin and smooth the surface. Set aside to cool.

3 Heat the olive oil in a frying pan. Add the onion and garlic and fry over a medium heat, stirring occasionally, for about 3–5 minutes, until soft. Add the tomatoes, tomato purée and sugar. Season to taste with salt and pepper. Reduce the heat and simmer for 20 minutes. Meanwhile, preheat the oven to 200°C/400°F/Gas 6.

4 Turn out the polenta on to a chopping board and cut it into 5cm/2in squares. Place half the squares in the prepared ovenproof dish. Spoon over half the tomato sauce, and sprinkle with half the grated cheese. Repeat the layers. Bake for about 25 minutes, until golden.

stuffed tomatoes & peppers

COLOURFUL PEPPERS AND **TOMATOES** MAKE PERFECT **CONTAINERS** FOR VARIOUS **VEGETABLE STUFFINGS**. THIS **RICE** AND **HERB** VERSION USES **TYPICALLY GREEK** INGREDIENTS.

ingredients

2 large ripe **tomatoes**

1 **green pepper**

1 **yellow** or **orange pepper**

60ml/4 tbsp **olive oil**, plus extra
    for sprinkling

2 **onions**, chopped

2 **garlic cloves**, crushed

50g/2oz/½ cup **blanched
    almonds**, chopped

75g/3oz/scant ½ cup **long grain
    rice**, boiled and drained

15g/½oz fresh **mint**,
    roughly chopped

15g/½oz fresh **parsley**,
    roughly chopped

25g/1oz/2 tbsp **sultanas**

45ml/3 tbsp **ground almonds**

salt and freshly ground
    black pepper

chopped fresh **mixed herbs**,
    to garnish

method

SERVES 4

1 Preheat the oven to 190°C/375°F/Gas 5. Cut the tomatoes in half and scoop out the pulp and seeds using a teaspoon. Leave the tomatoes to drain on kitchen paper with cut sides down. Roughly chop the tomato pulp and seeds.

2 Halve the peppers, leaving the cores intact. Scoop out the seeds. Brush the peppers with 15ml/1 tbsp of the oil, place on a baking tray and bake for 15 minutes. Place the peppers and tomatoes in a shallow ovenproof dish and season to taste with salt and pepper.

3 Heat the remaining oil in a frying pan. Add the onions and fry over a medium heat, stirring occasionally, for 5 minutes. Add the garlic and chopped almonds and fry for 1 further minute.

4 Remove the pan from the heat and stir in the rice, chopped tomatoes, mint, parsley and sultanas. Season well with salt and pepper and spoon the mixture into the tomatoes and peppers.

5 Pour 150ml/¼ pint/⅔ cup boiling water around the tomatoes and peppers and bake, uncovered, for 20 minutes. Scatter with the ground almonds and sprinkle with a little extra olive oil. Return to the oven and bake for a further 20 minutes, or until turning golden. Serve immediately, garnished with fresh herbs, or allow to cool to room temperature to serve.

---

variation

Small aubergines or large courgettes also make good vegetables for stuffing. Halve and scoop out the centres of the vegetables, then oil the vegetable cases and bake for about 15 minutes. Chop the centres, fry for 2–3 minutes to soften and add to the stuffing mixture. Fill the aubergine or courgette cases with the stuffing and bake as for the peppers and tomatoes.

FRITTATA IS LIKE A **LARGE OMELETTE** – THIS TASTY VERSION IS **FILLED** WITH **POTATOES** AND **PLENTY** OF **HERBS**. DO USE **FRESH MINT** IN **PREFERENCE** TO DRIED IF YOU CAN FIND IT.

ingredients

450g/1lb small **new** or
   salad potatoes
6 **eggs**
30ml/2 tbsp chopped fresh **mint**
30ml/2 tbsp **olive oil**
1 **onion**, chopped
2 **garlic** cloves, crushed
2 **red peppers**, seeded and
   roughly chopped
salt and freshly ground
   black pepper
mint sprigs, to garnish

cook's tip
This will make a substantial dish for two people, using five or six eggs. If preferred, the frittata could be cooked as individual portions.

potato & red pepper frittata

method

SERVES 3–4

1 Cook the potatoes in their skins in boiling, lightly salted water until just tender. Drain and leave until cool enough to handle. Cut the potatoes into thick slices.

2 Whisk together the eggs, mint and seasoning in a bowl, then set aside. Heat the oil in a large frying pan.

3 Add the onion, garlic, peppers and potatoes to the pan and cook, stirring occasionally, for 5 minutes.

4 Pour the egg mixture over the vegetables in the frying pan and stir gently until just mixed.

5 Push the mixture towards the centre of the pan as it cooks to allow the liquid egg to run on to the base. Meanwhile preheat the grill.

6 When the frittata is lightly set, place the pan under the hot grill for 2–3 minutes, until the top is golden brown.

7 Serve hot or cold, cut into wedges and piled high on a serving dish, garnished with sprigs of mint.

chilli cheese tortilla with fresh tomato salsa

JUST AS **GOOD** SERVED **WARM** OR **COLD**, THIS TORTILLA IS LIKE A **SLICED POTATO QUICHE** WITHOUT THE **PASTRY BASE**. THE **SALSA** CAN BE MADE **WITHOUT** THE **CHILLI** IF YOU **PREFER**.

method

SERVES 4

1 To make the salsa, put the tomatoes in a bowl and add the chopped chilli, garlic, coriander, lime juice and salt. Mix well and set aside.

2 Heat 15ml/1 tbsp of the oil in a large omelette pan over a low heat. Add the onion and jalapeños and fry gently, stirring once or twice, for 5 minutes, until softened. Add the cooked potato and fry over a low heat, stirring occasionally, for 5 minutes, until lightly browned, taking care to keep the slices whole.

3 Using a slotted spoon, transfer the vegetables to a warm plate. Wipe the pan with kitchen paper, then add the remaining oil and heat until really hot. Return the vegetables to the pan. Scatter the grated cheese over the top.

4 Pour the beaten eggs into the pan, making sure that they seep under the vegetables and cover the base. Cook the tortilla over a low heat, without stirring, until it is just set. Slide it out of the pan on to a dish and serve hot or cold, cut into wedges, garnished with fresh herbs and with the salsa on the side.

ingredients

45ml/3 tbsp **sunflower** or **olive oil**

1 small **onion**, thinly sliced

2–3 fresh **green jalapeño chillies**, seeded and sliced

200g/7oz cold cooked **potato**, thinly sliced

120g/4¼oz/generous 1 cup grated **cheese** (use a firm but not hard cheese, such as **Double Gloucester**, **Monterey Jack** or **Manchego**)

6 **eggs**, beaten

salt and freshly ground **black pepper**

fresh **herbs**, to garnish

For the salsa

500g/1¼lb fresh flavoursome **tomatoes**, peeled, seeded and finely chopped

1 fresh, mild **green chilli**, seeded and finely chopped

2 **garlic cloves**, crushed

45ml/3 tbsp chopped fresh **coriander**

juice of 1 **lime**

2.5ml/½ tsp **salt**

twice baked soufflés

THESE **LITTLE** SOUFFLÉS ARE **SERVED UPSIDE-DOWN**. THEY ARE **REMARKABLY EASY** TO MAKE AND CAN BE **PREPARED** UP TO A DAY **IN ADVANCE**, THEN **REHEATED** IN THE **SAUCE** – PERFECT FOR **EASY ENTERTAINING**.

ingredients

method

SERVES 6

20g/¾oz/1½ tbsp **butter**, plus
    extra for greasing
30ml/2 tbsp **plain flour**
150ml/¼ pint/⅔ cup **milk**
1 small **bay leaf**
freshly grated **nutmeg**
2 **eggs**, separated, plus 1 **egg
    white**, at room temperature
75g/3oz/¾ cup grated
    Gruyère cheese
1.5ml/¼ tsp **cream of tartar**
salt and freshly ground
    black pepper

For the tomato cream sauce
300ml/½ pint/1¼ cups
    whipping cream
10ml/2 tsp **tomato purée**
1 ripe **tomato**, peeled, seeded
    and finely diced
salt and **cayenne pepper**

1 Preheat the oven to 190°C/375°F/Gas 5. Generously butter six 175ml/6fl oz/¾ cup ramekins or dariole moulds, then line the bases with buttered greaseproof or non-stick baking parchment.

2 Melt the butter in a heavy-based saucepan over a medium heat. Stir in the flour and cook, stirring constantly, until just golden. Pour in about half the milk, whisking vigorously until smooth, then whisk in the remaining milk and add the bay leaf. Season with a little salt and plenty of pepper and nutmeg. Bring to the boil and cook, stirring constantly, for about 1 minute.

3 Remove the sauce from the heat and discard the bay leaf. Beat the egg yolks, one at a time, into the hot sauce, then stir in the cheese until it is melted. Set aside.

4 In a large, clean grease-free bowl, whisk the egg whites slowly until they become frothy. Add the cream of tartar, then increase the speed and whisk until they form peaks that just flop over at the top.

5 Whisk a spoonful of beaten egg whites into the cheese sauce to lighten it. Pour the cheese sauce over the remaining whites. Using a rubber spatula or large metal spoon, gently fold the sauce into the whites with a figure-of-eight movement.

6 Spoon the soufflé mixture into the prepared ramekins or dariole moulds, filling them about three-quarters full. Put the dishes in a shallow ovenproof dish or roasting tin and pour in boiling water to come halfway up the sides of the dishes. Bake for about 18 minutes, until puffed up and golden brown. Let the soufflés cool in the dishes long enough to deflate.

7 To make the sauce, bring the cream just to the boil in a small saucepan. Reduce the heat, stir in the tomato purée and diced tomato and cook for 2–3 minutes. Season to taste with salt and cayenne pepper. Spoon a thin layer of sauce into a gratin dish just large enough to hold the soufflés. Run a knife around the edge of the soufflés and invert to unmould. Remove the lining paper if necessary. Pour the remaining sauce over the soufflés and bake for about 12–15 minutes until well browned.

A **COMBINATION** OF **VEGETABLES** AND FRESH **HERBS**, **LAYERED** AND **BAKED** IN A **SPINACH-LINED LOAF** TIN. THIS WOULD BE PERFECTLY **DELICIOUS** SERVED **HOT** OR **WARM** WITH A SIMPLE **SALAD GARNISH**.

ingredients

3 **red peppers**, halved

450g/1lb **waxy potatoes**

115g/4oz **spinach**
    leaves, trimmed

25g/1oz/2 tbsp **butter**

pinch of grated **nutmeg**

115g/4oz/1 cup grated
    Cheddar cheese

1 medium **courgette**, sliced
    lengthways and blanched

salt and freshly ground
    black pepper

lettuce and **tomatoes**,
    to serve

layered vegetable terrine

method

SERVES 6

1 Preheat the oven to 180°C/350°F/Gas 4. Place the peppers in a roasting tin and roast, with the cores in place, for 30–45 minutes, until charred. Remove from the oven. Place in a plastic bag to cool and tie the top. When cool, peel the skins and remove the cores. Cut the potatoes in half and boil in lightly salted water for 10–15 minutes.

2 Blanch the spinach for a few seconds in boiling water. Drain thoroughly and pat dry on kitchen paper. Use to line the base and sides of a 900g/2lb loaf tin, making sure the leaves overlap slightly.

3 Slice the potatoes thinly and arrange one-third of the slices over the base of the loaf tin. Dot with a little of the butter and season to taste with salt, pepper and nutmeg. Sprinkle over a little of the grated Cheddar cheese.

4 Arrange three of the peeled pepper halves on top. Sprinkle over a little grated cheese, and then add a layer of courgette slices. Place half the remaining potatoes on top, together with the remaining peppers and some more cheese, seasoning as you go. Arrange the final layer of potato slices on top and scatter over any remaining cheese. Fold the spinach leaves over, then cover with foil.

5 Place the loaf tin in a roasting tin and pour boiling water around the outside, making sure the water comes halfway up the sides of the loaf tin. Bake for 45 minutes–1 hour. Remove from the oven and turn out the loaf. Serve in slices, with lettuce and tomatoes.

baked scalloped
potatoes with feta & olives

THINLY **SLICED POTATOES** ARE COOKED WITH CRUMBLED **GREEK FETA** CHEESE AND **BLACK** AND **GREEN OLIVES** IN OLIVE OIL. THIS DISH IS A GOOD ONE TO **SERVE** WITH TOASTED **PITTA BREAD**.

method

SERVES 4

1 Preheat the oven to 200°C/400°F/Gas 6. Cook the potatoes, in their skins, in plenty of boiling water for 15 minutes. Drain and set aside to cool slightly. Peel the potatoes and cut into thin slices.

2 Brush the base and sides of a 1.5 litre/2½ pint/6¼ cup rectangular ovenproof dish with some of the olive oil.

3 Layer the potatoes in the dish with the rosemary, cheese and olives. Drizzle with olive oil and pour the stock into the dish. Season with salt and plenty of pepper.

4 Bake for 35 minutes, covering the dish with foil part of the way through the cooking time to prevent the potatoes from getting too brown. Serve hot, straight from the dish, with pitta bread and olives.

ingredients

900g/2lb **potatoes**
150ml/¼ pint/⅔ cup **olive oil**
1 fresh **rosemary** sprig
275g/10oz Greek **feta cheese**, crumbled
115g/4oz/1 cup pitted **black** and **green olives**
300ml/½ pint/1¼ cups hot **vegetable stock**
salt and freshly ground **black pepper**
toasted pitta bread and **black** and **green olives**, to serve

cook's tip
Make sure you choose Greek feta cheese, which has a completely different texture from Danish, a widely available variety. Bulgarian feta is also excellent and is usually made from ewe's milk in the traditional way.

summer herb & ricotta flan

SIMPLE TO MAKE AND **INFUSED** WITH **AROMATIC** FRESH **BASIL, OREGANO** AND **CHIVES**, THIS **DELICATE** FLAN MAKES A **WONDERFUL** LUNCH **DISH**.

ingredients

750g/1lb 11oz/3½ cups
  ricotta cheese
75g/3oz/1 cup finely grated
  Parmesan cheese
3 **eggs**, separated
60ml/4 tbsp torn fresh **basil
  leaves**, plus a few extra
  leaves, to garnish
60ml/4 tbsp snipped
  fresh **chives**
45ml/3 tbsp fresh
  oregano leaves

2.5ml/½ tsp **salt**
2.5ml/½ tsp **paprika**
olive oil, for greasing
  and glazing
freshly ground **black pepper**

For the tapenade
400g/14oz/3½ cups pitted **black
  olives**, rinsed and halved,
  with a few **whole olives**
  reserved, to garnish (optional)
5 **garlic cloves**, crushed
75ml/5 tbsp/⅓ cup extra virgin
  olive oil

method

SERVES 4

1 Preheat the oven to 180°C/350°F/Gas 4 and lightly grease a 23cm/9in springform cake tin with oil. Mix together the ricotta, Parmesan and egg yolks in a food processor or blender. Add the herbs and salt, and season to taste with pepper. Process until the mixture is smooth and creamy.

2 Whisk the egg whites in a large bowl using a hand-held electric whisk until they form soft peaks. Gently fold the egg whites into the ricotta mixture with figure-of-eight movements, taking care not to knock out too much air. Spoon the ricotta mixture into the prepared tin and smooth the top.

3 Bake in the oven for 1 hour 20 minutes, or until the flan is risen and the top golden. Remove from the oven and brush lightly with olive oil, then sprinkle with paprika. Leave the flan to cool before removing it from the tin.

4 Make the tapenade. Place the olives and garlic in a food processor or blender and process until finely chopped. With the motor running, gradually add the olive oil and blend to a coarse paste. Transfer the tapenade to a serving bowl. Transfer the cooled flan to a serving plate, garnish with the basil leaves and olives, if using, and serve with the bowl of tapenade.

red onion & goat's cheese pastries

THESE **ATTRACTIVE** LITTLE **PASTRIES** COULDN'T BE **EASIER** TO MAKE. **RING THE CHANGES** BY **SPREADING** THE PASTRY BASE WITH **PESTO** OR **TAPENADE** BEFORE YOU **ADD** THE **FILLING**.

ingredients

15ml/1 tbsp **olive oil**
450g/1lb **red onions**, sliced
30ml/2 tbsp fresh **thyme** or
  10ml/2 tsp dried
15ml/1 tbsp **balsamic vinegar**
425g/15oz ready-rolled **puff
  pastry**, thawed if frozen

115g/4oz **goat's
  cheese**, cubed
1 **egg**, beaten
salt and freshly ground
  black pepper
fresh **thyme** sprigs, to
  garnish (optional)
mixed **green salad leaves**,
  to serve

method

SERVES 4

1 Heat the oil in a large heavy-based frying pan. Add the onions and fry over a low heat for 10 minutes, or until softened, stirring occasionally to prevent them from browning. Add the thyme and balsamic vinegar, season to taste with salt and pepper, and cook for a further 5 minutes. Remove the pan from the heat and set aside to cool.

2 Preheat the oven to 220°C/425°F/Gas 7. Unroll the pastry and using a 15cm/6in plate as a guide, cut four rounds. Place the pastry rounds on a dampened baking sheet and, using the point of a knife, score a border, 2cm/¾in inside the edge of each round.

3 Divide the onions among the pastry rounds and top with the goat's cheese. Brush the edge of each round with beaten egg and bake for 25–30 minutes, until golden. Garnish with thyme, if using, before serving with mixed green salad leaves.

---

cook's tip
Do not be tempted to rush the cooking of the onions. It is essential to cook them slowly over a low heat until they are sweet and tender. Stir frequently to prevent them from burning.

roasted squash

method

GEM SQUASH HAS A **SWEET SUBTLE** FLAVOUR THAT **CONTRASTS** WELL WITH THE **OLIVES** AND **SUN-DRIED TOMATOES**. THE **RICE** ADDS **SUBSTANCE** WITHOUT **CHANGING** ANY OF THE **FLAVOURS**.

1 Preheat the oven to 180°C/350°F/Gas 4. Trim away the base of each squash, slice off the top and, using a spoon, scoop out and discard the seeds.

2 Mix together the rice, tomatoes, olives, cheese, half the olive oil and the chopped basil in a large bowl.

3 Brush a shallow ovenproof dish with the remaining oil, just large enough to hold the squash side by side. Divide the rice mixture between the squash and place them in the dish.

4 Cover with foil and bake for 45–50 minutes, until the squash is tender when pierced with a skewer. Garnish with basil sprigs and serve with a yogurt and mint dressing or with a green salad.

ingredients

4 whole **gem squash**

225g/8oz/1⅓ cups cooked **white long grain rice**

75g/3oz/¾ cup **sun-dried tomatoes**, chopped

50g/2oz/½ cup pitted **black olives**, chopped

60ml/4 tbsp soft **goat's cheese**

30ml/2 tbsp **olive oil**

15ml/1 tbsp chopped fresh **basil leaves**, plus fresh **basil sprigs**, to garnish

yogurt and **mint dressing** or **green salad**, to serve

cook's tip

To make a yogurt and mint dressing, beat together 150ml/¼ pint/⅔ cup natural yogurt, the juice of ½ lemon and 45–60ml/3–4 tbsp finely chopped fresh mint and season to taste with freshly ground black pepper.

PEPPERY ROCKET AND **AROMATIC** FRESH **BASIL** ADD BOTH **COLOUR** AND **FLAVOUR** TO THIS CRISP **PIZZA**.

ingredients

10ml/2 tsp **olive oil**, plus extra
   for drizzling
1 **garlic clove**, crushed
150g/5oz/1 cup canned
   chopped **tomatoes**
2.5ml/½ tsp **sugar**
30ml/2 tbsp torn fresh
   basil leaves
2 **tomatoes**, seeded
   and chopped
150g/5oz **mozzarella**
   cheese, sliced
20g/¾oz/1 cup **rocket leaves**
rock salt and freshly ground
   black pepper

For the pizza base
225g/8oz/2 cups **strong white**
   flour, sifted
5ml/1 tsp **salt**
2.5ml/½ tsp **easy-blend**
   dried yeast
15ml/1 tbsp **olive oil**

method

SERVES 2

1 To make the pizza base, place the flour, salt and yeast in a bowl. Make a well in the centre and add the oil and 150ml/¼ pint/⅔ cup warm water. Mix with a round-bladed knife to form a soft dough.

2 Turn out on to a lightly floured work surface and knead for 5 minutes. Cover and leave to rest for 5 minutes, then knead for 5 minutes more until smooth and elastic. Place in a lightly oiled bowl and cover with clear film. Leave in a warm place for 45 minutes, until doubled in bulk.

3 Preheat the oven to 220°C/425°F/Gas 7. Make the topping. Heat the oil in a frying pan. Add the garlic and fry over a low heat, stirring constantly, for 1 minute. Add the canned chopped tomatoes and sugar and cook, stirring occasionally, for 5–7 minutes, until reduced and thickened. Stir in the basil, season to taste with salt and pepper, then set aside.

4 Knead the risen dough lightly, then roll out to form a rough 30cm/12in round. Place on a lightly oiled baking sheet and push up the edges of the dough to form a shallow, even rim.

5 Spoon the tomato mixture evenly over the pizza base, then top with the chopped fresh tomatoes. Arrange the slices of mozzarella on top. Season with rock salt and pepper and drizzle with a little olive oil. Bake in the oven for 10–12 minutes, until crisp and golden. Scatter the rocket over the pizza just before serving.

main dinners

ingredients

225g/8oz/1¼ cups **dried black beans**

1 **bay leaf**

30ml/2 tbsp **vegetable oil**

1 large **onion**, chopped

1 **garlic clove**, chopped

5ml/1 tsp **English mustard powder**

15ml/1 tbsp **blackstrap molasses**

30ml/2 tbsp **dark brown sugar**

5ml/1 tsp dried **thyme**

2.5ml/½ tsp dried **chilli flakes**

5ml/1 tsp **vegetable bouillon powder**

1 **red pepper**, seeded and diced

1 **yellow pepper**, seeded and diced

675g/1½lb **butternut squash** or **pumpkin**, seeded and cut into 1cm/½in dice

salt and freshly ground **black pepper**

fresh **thyme** sprigs, to garnish

jamaican black bean hot pot

MOLASSES IMPARTS A RICH **TREACLY FLAVOUR** TO THE **SPICY SAUCE**, WHICH INCORPORATES A **STUNNING MIX** OF **BLACK BEANS**, VIBRANT RED AND YELLOW **PEPPERS** AND ORANGE **BUTTERNUT SQUASH**. SERVE WITH **CORNBREAD** OR **PLAIN BOILED RICE**.

method

SERVES 2–4

1 Soak the beans overnight in plenty of water, then drain and rinse well. Place in a large saucepan, cover with fresh water and add the bay leaf. Bring to the boil, then boil rapidly for 10 minutes. Reduce the heat, cover and simmer for 30 minutes, until tender. Drain, reserving the cooking water. Preheat the oven to 180°C/350°F/Gas 4.

2 Heat the oil in a saucepan. Add the onion and garlic and sauté over a low heat, stirring occasionally, for 5 minutes, until softened. Add the mustard powder, molasses, sugar, dried thyme and chilli flakes and cook, stirring constantly, for 1 minute. Stir in the black beans and spoon the mixture into a flameproof casserole.

3 Add water to the reserved cooking liquid to make 400ml/14fl oz/ 1⅔ cups, then stir in the bouillon powder until completely dissolved. Pour into the casserole, cover and bake for 25 minutes.

4 Add the peppers and squash or pumpkin and mix well. Cover the casserole and bake for a further 45 minutes, until the vegetables are tender. Serve immediately, garnished with thyme.

cook's tip
Molasses is the residue left after sugar cane has been refined. It has a very rich flavour and is less sweet than most other syrups. The darkest variety, which has a slightly bitter aftertaste, is known as blackstrap molasses. It is a traditional ingredient in bean dishes in both North America and the Caribbean.

mixed mushroom lasagne

THIS **SIMPLE** VEGETARIAN **VERSION** OF THE **UBIQUITOUS LASAGNE** REQUIRES **NO** LENGTHY **PREPARATION** OF VARIOUS SAUCES AND FILLINGS, BUT **TASTES** JUST AS **GOOD** AS MORE TRADITIONAL VERSIONS.

method

SERVES 4

1 Place the porcini mushrooms in a bowl and cover with boiling water. Set aside to soak for 15 minutes, then drain and rinse.

2 Heat the oil in a large heavy-based frying pan. Add the soaked mushrooms and sauté over a high heat for 5 minutes, until the edges are crisp. Reduce the heat, then add the garlic and fresh mushrooms and sauté, stirring occasionally, for a further 5 minutes, until tender.

3 Add the wine and cook for 5–7 minutes, until reduced. Stir in the tomatoes and sugar and season to taste with salt and pepper. Cook over a medium heat for about 5 minutes, until thickened.

4 Meanwhile, cook the sheets of lasagne according to the instructions on the packet until it is tender, but still firm to the bite. Drain lightly: the pasta should still be moist.

5 To serve, spoon a little of the sauce on to each of four warm serving plates. Place a sheet of lasagne on top and spoon a quarter of the mushroom sauce over each serving. Sprinkle with some Parmesan and top with another pasta sheet. Sprinkle with black pepper and more Parmesan and garnish with basil leaves. Serve immediately.

ingredients

40g/1½oz/⅔ cup dried
porcini mushrooms
50ml/2fl oz/¼ cup **olive oil**
1 large **garlic clove**, chopped
375g/13oz/5 cups **mixed mushrooms**, including **brown cap**, **field**, **shiitake** and **wild varieties**, roughly sliced
175ml/6fl oz/¾ cup dry **white wine**
90ml/6 tbsp canned chopped **tomatoes**
2.5ml/½ tsp **sugar**
8 fresh **lasagne sheets**
40g/1½oz/½ cup freshly grated **Parmesan cheese**
salt and freshly ground **black pepper**
fresh **basil leaves**, to garnish

pappardelle with olive & caper paste

THIS **HOME-MADE** PASTA IS **FLAVOURED** WITH **SUN-DRIED TOMATO** PASTE, AND THE RESULTS ARE **WELL WORTH** THE EFFORT, BUT **BOUGHT PASTA** CAN BE **SUBSTITUTED** FOR A **REALLY QUICK** SUPPER **DISH**.

method

SERVES 4

1 To make the pasta, sift the flour and salt into a bowl and make a well in the centre. Lightly beat the eggs with the tomato paste and pour the mixture into the well.

2 Mix the ingredients together using a round-bladed knife. Turn out on to a work surface and knead for 6–8 minutes, until the dough is very smooth and soft, working in a little more flour if it becomes sticky. Wrap in aluminium foil and chill for 30 minutes.

3 To make the sauce, put the olives, capers, anchovies, chilli, basil and parsley in a food processor or blender, together with the oil. Process very briefly until the ingredients are finely chopped. (Alternatively, you can finely chop the ingredients and then mix with the olive oil.)

4 Plunge the tomatoes into boiling water for 30 seconds, then refresh in cold water. Peel the skins, remove the seeds and dice. Roll out the dough very thinly on a floured surface. Sprinkle with a little flour, then roll up like a Swiss roll. Cut across into 1cm/½in slices.

5 Unroll the pasta strips and lay out on a clean dish towel for about 10 minutes to dry out.

6 Bring a large saucepan of salted water to the boil. Add the pasta and cook for 2–3 minutes, until just tender. Drain immediately and return to the saucepan.

7 Add the olive mixture and tomatoes and season with salt and pepper to taste, then toss together gently over a moderate heat for about 1 minute, until heated through. Garnish with fresh basil and serve scattered with shavings of fresh Parmesan.

ingredients

For the pasta
275g/10oz/2½ cups **plain white flour**
1.5ml/¼ tsp **salt**
3 medium **eggs**
45ml/3 tbsp **sun-dried tomato paste**

For the sauce
115g/4oz/1 cup pitted **black olives**
75ml/5 tbsp **capers**
5 drained **anchovy fillets**
1 **red chilli**, seeded and roughly chopped
60ml/4 tbsp roughly chopped fresh **basil**, plus extra to garnish
60ml/4 tbsp roughly chopped fresh **parsley**
150ml/¼ pint/⅔ cup **olive oil**
4 ripe **tomatoes**
salt and freshly ground **black pepper**
Parmesan cheese shavings, to serve

ingredients

40g/1½oz/3 tbsp **butter**

1 small **onion**, finely chopped

1.2 litres/2 pints/5 cups
vegetable stock

350g/12oz/1¾ cups **arborio** or
other **risotto rice**

200ml/7fl oz/scant 1 cup dry
white wine

50g/2oz/½ cup grated
Gruyère cheese

50g/2oz/½ cup diced
taleggio cheese

50g/2oz/½ cup diced
Gorgonzola cheese

50g/2oz/⅔ cup freshly grated
Parmesan cheese

salt and freshly ground
black pepper

chopped fresh **flat leaf parsley**,
to garnish

cook's tip
Only ever use a risotto rice for a
risotto. The round grains absorb a
large amount of liquid to give risotto
its characteristic creamy texture.
Arborio, carnaroli, vialone nano, roma
and baldo are the most commonly
available risotto rices.

risotto with four cheeses

THIS **RICH DISH** WILL SERVE FOUR AS A
MAIN MEAL, OR SIX FOR A **DINNER PARTY
FIRST COURSE**, WITH A **SPARKLING WINE**.

method
SERVES 4–6

1 Melt the butter in a large heavy-based saucepan or deep frying pan.
Add the onion and fry over a low heat, stirring frequently, for about
4–5 minutes, until softened but not browned. Pour the stock into
another pan and heat it to simmering point.

2 Add the rice to the onion mixture, stir until the grains start to swell and
burst, then add the wine. Stir until it stops sizzling and most of it has
been absorbed by the rice, then pour in a little of the hot stock.
Season with salt and pepper to taste. Stir over a low heat until the
stock has been absorbed.

3 Gradually add the remaining stock, a little at a time, allowing the rice
to absorb the liquid before adding more, and stirring constantly. After
20–25 minutes the rice will be tender with a slight "bite" and the
risotto will be creamy.

4 Turn off the heat under the pan, then add the grated Gruyère, diced
taleggio, diced Gorgonzola and 30ml/2 tbsp of the grated Parmesan.
Stir gently until the cheeses have melted, then taste for seasoning and
adjust if necessary. Transfer the risotto to a warm serving bowl and
garnish with chopped flat leaf parsley. Serve immediately and hand the
remaining Parmesan separately.

spiced vegetable couscous

COUSCOUS, A CEREAL PROCESSED FROM **SEMOLINA**, IS USED THROUGHOUT **NORTH AFRICA**. IT IS ESPECIALLY POPULAR IN **MOROCCO**, WHERE IT IS **SERVED** WITH MANY DISHES, INCLUDING **VEGETABLE STEWS** AND **TAGINES**.

ingredients

45ml/3 tbsp **vegetable oil**

1 large **onion**, finely chopped

2 **garlic** cloves, crushed

15ml/1 tbsp **tomato purée**

2.5ml/½ tsp **ground turmeric**

2.5ml/½ tsp **cayenne pepper**

5ml/1 tsp **ground coriander**

5ml/1 tsp **ground cumin**

225g/8oz/1½ cups
   cauliflower florets

225g/8oz **baby carrots**

1 **red pepper**, seeded and diced

4 **beefsteak tomatoes**

225g/8oz **courgettes**,
   thickly sliced

400g/14oz can **chick-peas**,
   drained and rinsed

45ml/3 tbsp chopped
   fresh **coriander**

salt and freshly ground
   black pepper

fresh **coriander sprigs**,
   to garnish

For the couscous

5ml/1 tsp **salt**

450g/1lb/2⅔ cups **couscous**

50g/2oz/2 tbsp **butter**

method

SERVES 6

1 Heat 30ml/2 tbsp of the oil in a large heavy-based saucepan. Add the onion and garlic and cook over a low heat, stirring occasionally, until soft. Stir in the tomato purée, turmeric, cayenne, ground coriander and cumin. Cook, stirring constantly, for 2 minutes.

2 Add the cauliflower florets, whole baby carrots and red pepper, with enough water to come halfway up the vegetables. Bring to the boil, then lower the heat, cover and simmer for 10 minutes.

3 Plunge the tomatoes into boiling water for 30 seconds, then refresh in cold water. Peel the skins and chop the flesh. Add the sliced courgettes, chick-peas and tomatoes to the other vegetables and cook for a further 10 minutes. Stir in the fresh coriander and season to taste with salt and pepper. Keep hot.

4 To cook the couscous, bring 475ml/16fl oz/2 cups water to the boil in a large saucepan. Add the remaining oil and the salt. Remove from the heat, and add the couscous, stirring constantly. Allow to swell for 2 minutes, then add the butter and heat through gently, stirring lightly to separate the grains.

5 Turn the couscous out on to a warm serving dish and spoon the vegetables on top, pouring over any liquid. Garnish with fresh coriander sprigs and serve immediately.

cook's tip
Beefsteak tomatoes have an excellent flavour and are ideal for this recipe, but you can substitute six ordinary tomatoes or two 400g/14oz cans chopped tomatoes. Sun-ripened tomatoes invariably have a richer, more concentrated flavour than those grown under glass.

ingredients

5ml/1 tsp **saffron strands**

40g/1½oz/½ cup **pine nuts**

45ml/3 tbsp **olive oil**

1 large **onion**, chopped

3 **garlic cloves**, crushed

1.5ml/¼ tsp **ground allspice**

4cm/1½in piece of fresh **root
   ginger**, grated

225g/8oz/generous 1 cup **long
   grain rice**

300ml/½ pint/1¼ cups
   vegetable stock

50g/2oz/½ cup **pickled
   walnuts**, drained and
   roughly chopped

40g/1½oz/¼ cup **raisins**

45ml/3 tbsp roughly chopped
   fresh **parsley** or **coriander**,
   plus extra to garnish

salt and freshly ground
   black pepper

natural yogurt, to serve

cook's tip

Use one small aubergine, finely
chopped and lightly fried in a little
olive oil, instead of the pickled
walnuts, if you prefer.

pilaff with saffron & pickled walnuts

PICKLED WALNUTS HAVE A **WARM, TANGY** FLAVOUR THAT GOES WELL WITH **RICE** AND **BULGUR WHEAT** DISHES. THIS **EASTERN MEDITERRANEAN** PILAFF IS **INTERESTING** ENOUGH TO **SERVE** ON ITS **OWN**, OR WITH **GRILLED** VEGETABLES.

method

SERVES 4

1 Put the saffron in a bowl with 15ml/1 tbsp boiling water and leave to stand. Heat a large frying pan and dry fry the pine nuts until they turn golden. Set them aside.

2 Heat the oil in the pan and fry the onion, garlic and allspice for 3 minutes. Stir in the ginger and rice and cook for 1 minute more.

3 Add the stock and bring to the boil. Reduce the heat, cover and simmer gently for 15 minutes, until the rice is just tender.

4 Stir in the saffron and soaking liquid, the pine nuts, pickled walnuts, raisins and parsley or coriander. Season to taste with salt and pepper. Heat through gently for 2 minutes. Transfer to a warm serving dish, garnish with parsley or coriander leaves and serve with natural yogurt.

turkish-style new potato casserole

HERE'S A **MEAL** IN A **POT** THAT'S SUITABLE FOR FEEDING **LARGE NUMBERS** OF **GUESTS**. IT'S **LIGHTLY SPICED** AND VERY **WELL GARLICKED** – WHO COULD **REFUSE**?

method

SERVES 4

1 Preheat the oven to 190°C/375°F/Gas 5. Heat 45ml/3 tbsp of the oil in a heavy-based pan. Add the onion and fry until golden.

2 Add the aubergines, sauté for about 3 minutes and then add the courgettes, peppers, peas, beans and potatoes. Stir in the cinnamon, cumin and paprika and season to taste with salt and pepper. Cook, stirring constantly, for 3 minutes. Transfer to a shallow ovenproof dish.

3 Halve, seed and chop the fresh tomatoes and mix with the canned tomatoes, parsley, garlic and the remaining olive oil in a bowl.

4 Pour the stock over the aubergine mixture and then spoon over the tomato mixture. Cover and bake for 30–45 minutes, until the vegetables are tender. Serve hot, garnished with black olives and fresh parsley.

ingredients

60ml/4 tbsp **olive oil**

1 large **onion**, chopped

2 small to medium **aubergines**, cut into small cubes

4 **courgettes**, cut into small chunks

1 **green pepper**, seeded and chopped

1 **red** or **yellow pepper**, seeded and chopped

115g/4oz/1 cup fresh or frozen **peas**

115g/4oz **French beans**

450g/1lb **new** or **salad potatoes**, cubed

2.5ml/½ tsp **ground cinnamon**

2.5ml/½ tsp **ground cumin**

5ml/1 tsp **paprika**

4–5 **tomatoes**, peeled

400g/14oz can chopped **tomatoes**

30ml/2 tbsp chopped fresh **parsley**

3–4 **garlic cloves**, crushed

350ml/12fl oz/1½ cups **vegetable stock**

salt and freshly ground **black pepper**

black olives and fresh **parsley**, to garnish

vegetable stir-fry with eggs

A PERFECT **FAMILY SUPPER** DISH, THIS IS **VERY EASY** TO **PREPARE**. SERVE WITH **PLENTY** OF **CRUSTY BREAD**: ITALIAN CIABATTA IS **PARTICULARLY GOOD**.

ingredients

30ml/2 tbsp **olive oil**

1 **onion**, roughly chopped

2 **garlic cloves**, crushed

225g/8oz **courgettes**

1 **red pepper**, seeded and
thinly sliced

1 **yellow pepper**, seeded and
thinly sliced

10ml/2 tsp **paprika**

400g/14oz can
chopped **tomatoes**

15ml/1 tbsp **sun-dried tomato
paste** or **tomato purée**

4 **eggs**

115g/4oz/1 cup grated
Cheddar cheese

salt and freshly ground
black pepper

fresh crusty **bread**, to serve

method

SERVES 4

1 Heat the oil in a deep, heavy-based frying pan. Add the onion and garlic and fry over a medium heat, stirring frequently, for 4 minutes, until beginning to soften.

2 Cut the courgettes into 5cm/2in long batons or strips. Add the courgettes and red and yellow peppers to the onion and cook gently, stirring frequently, for 3–4 minutes, until the vegetables are beginning to soften.

3 Stir in the paprika, tomatoes and sun-dried tomato paste or tomato purée and season to taste with salt and pepper. Bring to the boil, lower the heat and simmer gently for 15 minutes, or until the vegetables are just tender.

4 Reduce the heat to low. Make four wells in the vegetable mixture, break an egg into each well and season to taste with salt and pepper. Cook over a gentle heat until the egg whites begin to set.

5 Preheat the grill to hot. Sprinkle the cheese over the mixture in the pan. Protect the pan handle with foil if necessary. Cook under the grill for about 5 minutes, until the cheese is golden and the eggs are lightly set. Serve at once with plenty of crusty bread.

variation

This dish can also be baked in the oven. Follow the recipe for steps 1 and 2, then add the paprika, tomatoes and sun-dried tomato paste or tomato purée. Season with salt and pepper. Transfer the vegetable mixture to a greased ovenproof dish and bake in a preheated oven at 180°C/350°F/Gas 4 for 40 minutes. Make four wells in the mixture, break an egg into each and season. Return the dish to the oven and bake for a further 10 minutes. Sprinkle over the grated cheese and bake for 5 minutes more. Serve hot, straight from the dish.

thai vegetable curry with lemon grass rice

FRAGRANT JASMINE RICE, SUBTLY **FLAVOURED** WITH **LEMON GRASS** AND **CARDAMOM**, IS THE PERFECT ACCOMPANIMENT TO THIS **RICHLY SPICED** VEGETABLE **CURRY**. DON'T BE PUT OFF BY THE **LONG LIST** OF **INGREDIENTS**: THIS CURRY IS **VERY SIMPLE** TO MAKE.

ingredients

10ml/2 tsp **vegetable oil**

400ml/14fl oz/1⅔ cups **coconut milk**

300ml/½ pint/1¼ cups **vegetable stock**

225g/8oz **new potatoes**, halved or quartered, if large

130g/4½oz **baby corn cobs**

5ml/1 tsp **golden caster sugar**

185g/6½oz **broccoli florets**

1 **red pepper**, seeded and sliced lengthways

115g/4oz **spinach**, tough stalks removed and leaves shredded

30ml/2 tbsp chopped fresh **coriander**

salt and freshly ground **black pepper**

For the spice paste

1 **red chilli**, seeded and chopped

3 **green chillies**, seeded and chopped

1 **lemon grass stalk**, outer leaves removed and inside finely chopped

2 **shallots**, chopped

finely grated rind of 1 **lime**

2 **garlic cloves**, chopped

5ml/1 tsp ground **coriander**

2.5ml/½ tsp **ground cumin**

1cm/½in piece of fresh **galangal**, finely chopped or 2.5ml/½ tsp dried (optional)

30ml/2 tbsp chopped fresh **coriander**

15ml/1 tbsp chopped fresh **coriander roots** and **stems** (optional)

For the rice

225g/8oz/generous 1 cup **jasmine rice**, rinsed

1 **lemon grass stalk**, outer leaves removed and cut into 3 pieces

6 **cardamom pods**, bruised

method

SERVES 4

1 First, make the spice paste. Place all the ingredients in a food processor or blender and process until a coarse paste is formed.

2 Heat the oil in a large heavy-based saucepan. Add the spice paste and fry over a medium heat, stirring constantly, for 1–2 minutes. Add the coconut milk and stock and bring to the boil.

3 Reduce the heat, add the potatoes and simmer for 15 minutes. Add the baby corn and season to taste with salt and pepper, then cook for 2 minutes. Stir in the sugar, broccoli and red pepper and cook for 2 minutes more, until the vegetables are tender. Stir in the spinach, and half the fresh coriander. Cook for 2 minutes.

4 Meanwhile, prepare the rice. Tip the rinsed rice into a saucepan and add the lemon grass and cardamom pods. Pour over 475ml/16fl oz/2 cups water.

5 Bring to the boil, then reduce the heat, cover, and cook for 10–15 minutes, until the water is absorbed and the rice is tender and slightly sticky. Season with salt, leave to stand for 10 minutes, then fluff up the rice with a fork. Remove the spices and serve the rice immediately with the curry, sprinkled with the remaining fresh coriander.

red-cooked tofu with chinese mushrooms

RED-COOKED IS A TERM APPLIED TO **CHINESE DISHES** PREPARED WITH **DARK SOY SAUCE**. THIS **TASTY** DISH CAN BE SERVED EITHER AS A **SIDE DISH** FOR SIX OR A **MAIN MEAL** FOR FOUR.

ingredients

225g/8oz **firm tofu**
45ml/3 tbsp **dark soy sauce**
30ml/2 tbsp **Chinese rice wine**
   or **medium-dry sherry**
10ml/2 tsp **dark brown sugar**
1 **garlic clove**, crushed
15ml/1 tbsp grated fresh
   root ginger
2.5ml/½ tsp **Chinese five-
   spice powder**
pinch of ground roasted
   Szechuan peppercorns
6 dried **Chinese black
   mushrooms**
5ml/1 tsp **cornflour**
30ml/2 tbsp **groundnut oil**
5–6 **spring onions**, white and
   green parts separately sliced
   into 2.5cm/1in lengths
small **basil leaves**, to garnish
rice noodles, to serve

method

SERVES 4

1 Drain the tofu, pat dry with kitchen paper and cut it into 2.5cm/1in cubes. Place the tofu cubes in a shallow dish.

2 In a small bowl, mix together the soy sauce, Chinese rice wine or sherry, sugar, garlic, ginger, five-spice powder and ground roasted Szechuan peppercorns to taste. Pour the marinade over the tofu, toss well to coat and set aside to marinate for about 30 minutes. Drain, reserving the marinade.

3 Meanwhile, put the dried black mushrooms in a small bowl, cover with warm water and set aside to soak for 20–30 minutes, until soft. Drain, reserving 90ml/6 tbsp of the soaking liquid. Squeeze out any excess liquid from the mushrooms. Remove and discard the tough stalks and slice the caps.

4 In a small bowl, blend the cornflour with the reserved marinade and the mushroom soaking liquid until smooth.

5 Heat the oil in a preheated wok. Add the tofu and gently stir-fry for 2–3 minutes, until evenly golden. Remove from the wok and set aside.

6 Add the mushrooms and the white parts of the spring onions to the wok and stir-fry for 2 minutes. Pour in the cornflour mixture and cook, stirring constantly, for 1 minute, until thickened.

7 Return the tofu to the wok and add the green parts of the spring onions. Simmer gently for 1–2 minutes. Serve at once with rice noodles and scattered with basil leaves.

salads & side dishes

feta, mint & potato salad

GREEK FETA CHEESE, YOGURT AND FRESH MINT COMBINE WITH WARM NEW POTATOES IN THIS REFRESHING AND SUBSTANTIAL SALAD, REMINISCENT OF WARM SUMMER DAYS IN THE AEGEAN.

ingredients

500g/1¼lb **potatoes**
(see cook's tip)
90g/3½oz Greek **feta cheese**, crumbled

For the dressing
250ml/8fl oz/1 cup Greek-style
natural yogurt

15g/½oz/½ cup fresh
mint leaves
30ml/2 tbsp **mayonnaise**
salt and freshly ground
black pepper

method

SERVES 4

1 Steam the potatoes over a saucepan of boiling water for about 20 minutes, until tender, then drain thoroughly and tip into a large serving bowl.

2 Meanwhile, make the dressing. Place the yogurt and mint in a food processor or blender and process for a few minutes, until the mint leaves are finely chopped. Transfer the dressing to a small bowl.

3 Stir in the mayonnaise and season to taste with salt and pepper. Spoon the dressing over the warm potatoes and scatter with the crumbled feta cheese. Serve immediately.

cook's tip
If you can, use pink fir apple potatoes for this dish. They have a smooth, waxy texture and retain their shape when cooked, which makes them ideal for salads. They have a delicious nutty flavour and, although maincrop, share many of the characteristics of new potatoes. Charlotte and other special salad potatoes could be used instead.

---

apple & beetroot red salad

BITTER LEAVES ARE COMPLEMENTED BY SWEET-FLAVOURED APPLES AND BEETROOT IN THIS SUMMER SALAD.

ingredients

50g/2oz/½ cup whole
unblanched almonds
2 **red apples**, cored and diced
juice of ½ **lemon**
115g/4oz/4 cups **red salad leaves**, such as **lollo rosso**, **oak leaf** and **radicchio**
200g/7oz cooked **beetroot** in
natural juice, sliced

For the dressing
30ml/2 tbsp **olive oil**
15ml/1 tbsp **walnut oil**
15ml/1 tbsp red or white
wine vinegar
salt and freshly ground
black pepper

method

SERVES 4

1 Dry fry the almonds in a heavy-based frying pan over a low heat, tossing frequently to prevent them from burning, for 2–3 minutes, or until golden all over. Remove from the pan and set aside.

2 To make the dressing, put the olive oil, walnut oil and wine vinegar into a bowl or screw-top jar. Season to taste with salt and pepper. Stir or shake thoroughly to combine.

3 Toss the apples in lemon juice to prevent them from browning, then place in a large bowl and add the salad leaves, beetroot and almonds. Pour over the dressing, toss gently to mix and serve immediately.

cook's tip
Always add dressing to salad leaves at the very last minute before serving. Once dressed, if left to stand, the leaves will become soggy, droopy, discoloured and unappetizing in every possible way.

halloumi & grape salad

IN **CENTRAL** AND **EASTERN EUROPE**, FIRM SALTY **HALLOUMI** CHEESE IS OFTEN SERVED FRIED FOR **BREAKFAST** OR **SUPPER**. IN THIS RECIPE IT IS TOSSED WITH **SWEET**, **JUICY GRAPES** WHICH **COMPLEMENT** THE **DISTINCTIVE**, SLIGHTLY **SALTY FLAVOUR**.

method

SERVES 4

1 To make the dressing, mix together the olive oil, lemon juice, sugar and seasoning. Stir in the thyme or dill and set aside. Meanwhile, toss together the salad leaves and the green and black grapes, then transfer the salad to a large serving plate.

2 Thinly slice the cheese. Heat the oil in a large frying pan. Add the cheese and fry briefly until turning golden on the underside. Turn with a fish slice and cook the other side.

3 Arrange the cheese over the salad. Pour over the dressing and garnish with dill or thyme. Serve immediately.

ingredients

For the dressing

60ml/4 tbsp **olive oil**

15ml/1 tbsp **lemon juice**

2.5ml/½ tsp **caster sugar**

salt and freshly ground
   black pepper

15ml/1 tbsp chopped fresh
   thyme or **dill**

For the salad

150g/5oz mixed green
   salad leaves

75g/3oz/¾ cup seedless
   green grapes

75g/3oz/¾ cup seedless
   black grapes

250g/9oz **halloumi cheese**

45ml/3 tbsp **olive oil**

fresh young **thyme leaves** or
   dill, to garnish

cook's tip
You can usually remove the seeds from grapes – if you haven't been able to buy a seedless variety – by squeezing them gently. Otherwise, cut the grapes in half and remove the seeds with the point of the knife.

THE SIMPLE **LEMON DRESSING** GIVES A **SHARP TANG** TO CREAMY **AVOCADO**, SWEET **RED ONIONS** AND CRISP **SPINACH**. GOLDEN **POLENTA CROÛTONS**, WITH THEIR **CRUNCHY** EXTERIOR AND ` **MELT-IN-THE-MOUTH** CENTRES, ADD A GOOD **CONTRAST**.

ingredients

1 large **red onion**, cut
    into wedges
300g/11oz/3 cups ready-made
    polenta, cut into 1cm/
    ½in cubes
olive oil, for brushing
225g/8oz **baby spinach** leaves
1 **avocado**, peeled, stoned
    and sliced
5ml/1 tsp **lemon** juice

For the dressing
60ml/4 tbsp **extra virgin
    olive oil**
juice of ½ **lemon**
salt and freshly ground
    black pepper

avocado, red onion & spinach salad

method

SERVES 4

1 Preheat the oven to 200°C/400°F/Gas 6. Place the onion wedges and polenta cubes on a lightly oiled baking sheet and bake, turning them often, for 25 minutes. Leave to cool slightly.

2 Meanwhile, make the dressing. Place the olive oil, lemon juice and salt and pepper to taste in a bowl or screw-top jar. Stir or shake thoroughly to combine.

3 Place the spinach leaves in a serving bowl. Toss the avocado in the lemon juice to prevent it from browning, then add to the spinach, together with the roasted onions.

4 Pour over the dressing and toss gently to combine. Sprinkle the polenta croûtons over the salad just before serving.

cook's tip
If you can't find ready-made polenta, you can make your own using instant polenta grains. Simply cook according to the packet instructions, then pour into a tray and leave to cool and set.

waldorf salad with cheese

A **MULTI-PURPOSE** SALAD THAT CAN BE SERVED EITHER AS A **SIDE DISH** OR AS A VEGETARIAN **MAIN COURSE**. THE SALAD IS BEST **MADE** THE **NIGHT BEFORE**, SO THAT IT CAN **MARINATE** BEFORE **SERVING**.

ingredients

3 **celery** sticks, thinly sliced
1 small **onion**, thinly sliced
1 **carrot**, coarsely grated
400g/14oz **white cabbage**
1 tart **apple**
2.5ml/½ tsp **caraway seeds**
50g/2oz/½ cup chopped **walnuts**
200g/7oz **Cheddar** or other **hard cheese**, cubed

For the dressing
45ml/3 tbsp **olive oil**
30ml/2 tbsp **sunflower oil**
45ml/3 tbsp **cider vinegar** or white **wine vinegar**
pinch of **sugar**
pinch of **mustard powder**
pinch of dried **tarragon**
salt and freshly ground **black pepper**

method

SERVES 4

1 Put the celery, onion and carrot in a large bowl. Cut the cabbage in quarters, remove and discard the core, then shred each quarter finely. Add the cabbage to the bowl. Grate the apple coarsely and add it to the bowl, together with the caraway seeds and chopped walnuts. Toss well to combine.

2 Whisk the dressing ingredients in a jug and season well with salt and pepper. Stir the dressing into the vegetable mixture and set aside for at least 1 hour, preferably overnight, to allow the flavours to blend together. Mix in the cubes of cheese, then spoon into a serving dish and serve at once.

cook's tip
For a colour contrast, try making this salad with red cabbage or a mixture of red and white cabbage. You could also use one red-skinned and one green-skinned apple, both for colour contrast and a fruitier flavour. Substitute toasted hazelnuts for the walnuts, if you like.

pear & parmesan salad

THIS IS A **GOOD STARTER** WHEN PEARS ARE AT THEIR **SEASONAL BEST**. **DRIZZLE** WITH A **POPPY-SEED** DRESSING AND **TOP** WITH **SHAVINGS** OF FRESH **PARMESAN**.

ingredients

4 just-ripe **dessert pears**
50g/2oz freshly grated **Parmesan cheese**
watercress, to garnish
water biscuits, to serve

For the dressing
30ml/2 tbsp **extra virgin olive oil**
15ml/1 tbsp **sunflower oil**
30ml/2 tbsp **cider vinegar** or white **wine vinegar**
2.5ml/½ tsp **light brown sugar**
pinch of dried **thyme**
15ml/1 tbsp **poppy seeds**
salt and freshly ground **black pepper**

method

SERVES 4

1 Cut the pears into quarters and remove the cores. Cut each pear quarter in half lengthways and arrange them on four small serving plates. Peel the pears if you wish, although they usually look more attractive unpeeled.

2 Make the dressing. Mix together the olive oil, sunflower oil, vinegar, sugar and thyme in a jug. Season to taste with salt and pepper, whisk thoroughly, then tip in the poppy seeds.

3 Trickle the dressing over the pears. Garnish with watercress and shave Parmesan over the top. Serve with water biscuits, if you like.

cook's tip
Blue cheeses also have a natural affinity with pears. Stilton, dolcelatte, Gorgonzola or Danish blue would all make good substitutes for Parmesan. Allow about 200g/7oz cheese, cut into wedges or cubes and sprinkled over the pears.

root vegetable gratin with spices

SUBTLY SPICED WITH **CURRY POWDER**, **TURMERIC**, **CORIANDER** AND **MILD CHILLI POWDER**, THIS **RICH GRATIN** IS **SUBSTANTIAL** ENOUGH TO SERVE ON ITS OWN FOR **LUNCH** OR **SUPPER**. IT ALSO MAKES A GOOD **ACCOMPANIMENT** TO A **VEGETABLE** OR **BEAN CURRY**.

method

SERVES 4

1 Thinly slice the potatoes, sweet potatoes and celeriac, using a sharp knife or the slicing attachment of a food processor. Immediately place the vegetables in a bowl of cold water to prevent discoloration.

2 Preheat the oven to 180°C/350°F/Gas 4. Melt half the butter in a heavy-based saucepan. Add the curry powder, turmeric and ground coriander and half the chilli powder. Cook, stirring constantly, for 2 minutes to allow the flavour of the spices to mingle. Remove the pan from the heat and set aside to cool slightly. Mix together the shallots, cream and milk, then add the spice mixture and stir well.

3 Drain the vegetables, then pat dry with kitchen paper. Arrange the vegetables in layers in a gratin dish, seasoning between each layer with salt and pepper. Pour the cream and spice mixture over the vegetables, then sprinkle with the remaining chilli powder. Cover with greaseproof paper and bake in the oven for 45 minutes.

4 Remove and discard the greaseproof paper. Dot the surface of the vegetables with the remaining butter and bake for a further 50 minutes, until golden. Serve immediately, garnished with chopped fresh flat leaf parsley.

ingredients

2 large **potatoes**, total weight about 450g/1lb

2 **sweet potatoes**, total weight about 275g/10oz

175g/6oz **celeriac**

15g/1 tbsp **unsalted butter**

5ml/1 tsp **curry powder**

5ml/1 tsp **ground turmeric**

2.5ml/½ tsp **ground coriander**

5ml/1 tsp mild **chilli powder**

3 **shallots**, chopped

150ml/¼ pint/⅔ cup **single cream**

150ml/¼ pint/⅔ cup **milk**

salt and freshly ground **black pepper**

chopped fresh **flat leaf parsley**, to garnish

ingredients

450g/1lb **baby
onions**, peeled

50ml/2fl oz/¼ cup white
wine vinegar

45ml/3 tbsp **olive oil**

40g/1½oz/3 tbsp
caster sugar

45ml/3 tbsp **tomato purée**

1 **bay leaf**

2 fresh **parsley** sprigs

65g/2½oz/½ cup **raisins**

salt and freshly ground
black pepper

fresh, crusty **bread**, to serve

cook's tip

To enjoy its full flavour, this dish is
best served at room temperature.
If it has to be stored in the fridge,
remove it at least half an hour before
serving. It would work very well as an
accompaniment to a vegetarian bake,
a cheese soufflé or a plain omelette,
and would be equally delicious as
part of a cold buffet with a selection
of cheeses, hard-boiled eggs,
tomatoes, salad leaves and a
vegetable terrine. Fresh, crusty bread
is virtually essential for mopping up
the scrumptious juices.

sweet & sour
onion salad

THIS RECIPE IS **PRIMARILY** FROM
PROVENCE, IN THE **SOUTH OF FRANCE**,
BUT THERE ARE **INFLUENCES** FROM OTHER
MEDITERRANEAN COUNTRIES, TOO.

method

SERVES 6

1   Put all ingredients except the bread in a pan with 300ml/½ pint/
1¼ cups water. Bring to the boil and simmer over a low heat,
uncovered, for about 45 minutes, or until the onions are tender
and most of the liquid has evaporated.

2   Remove and discard the bay leaf and parsley, check the seasoning,
and transfer to a serving dish. Set aside to cool to room temperature
before serving with fresh bread.

courgettes in rich tomato sauce

THIS **RICH-FLAVOURED MEDITERRANEAN** DISH CAN BE **SERVED HOT** OR **COLD**, EITHER AS A **SIDE DISH** OR AS PART OF A **TAPAS** MEAL. CUT THE **COURGETTES** INTO FAIRLY **THICK SLICES**, SO THAT THEY STAY SLIGHTLY **CRUNCHY**.

ingredients

15ml/1 tbsp **extra virgin olive oil**

1 **onion**, chopped

1 **garlic clove**, chopped

4 **courgettes**, thickly sliced

400g/14oz/3 cups canned **tomatoes**, strained

2 **tomatoes**, peeled, seeded and chopped

5ml/1 tsp **vegetable bouillon powder**

15ml/1 tbsp **tomato purée**

salt and freshly ground **black pepper**

method

SERVES 4

1 Heat the oil in a heavy-based saucepan. Add the onion and garlic and fry gently over a medium heat, stirring occasionally, for 5 minutes, or until the onion is softened.

2 Add the courgettes and cook, stirring occasionally, for a further 5 minutes, until beginning to colour.

3 Add the canned and fresh tomatoes, bouillon powder and tomato purée. Stir well, lower the heat and simmer for 10–15 minutes, until the sauce is reduced and thickened and the courgettes are just tender. Season to taste with salt and pepper, transfer to a warm serving dish and serve immediately.

cook's tip
For a more substantial dish and extra flavour, you could add 1 or 2 seeded and thickly sliced red peppers. Add them to the pan with the courgettes in step 2.

---

baked fennel with a crumb crust

THE DELICATE **ANISEED FLAVOUR** OF **BAKED** FENNEL MAKES IT A VERY **GOOD** SIDE DISH **ACCOMPANIMENT** TO ALL SORTS OF **PASTA** DISHES AND **RISOTTOS**.

ingredients

3 **fennel bulbs**, cut lengthways into quarters

30ml/2 tbsp extra virgin **olive oil**

1 **garlic** clove, chopped

50g/2oz/1 cup day-old **wholemeal breadcrumbs**

30ml/2 tbsp chopped fresh **flat leaf parsley**

salt and freshly ground **black pepper**

fennel leaves, to garnish (optional)

method

SERVES 4

1 Cook the fennel in a large saucepan of boiling lightly salted water for about 10 minutes, or until just tender.

2 Drain the fennel thoroughly and transfer to an ovenproof dish or roasting tin, then brush with half of the olive oil. Preheat the oven to 190°C/375°F/Gas 5.

3 In a small bowl, mix together the garlic, breadcrumbs and parsley, together with the remaining olive oil. Sprinkle the mixture evenly over the fennel, then season to taste with salt and pepper.

4 Bake in the oven for 30 minutes, or until the fennel is tender and the breadcrumb crust is crisp and golden. Serve hot, garnished with a few fennel leaves, if you wish.

cook's tip
For a light lunch or supper dish, you could add a finely chopped shallot that has been sautéed in a little olive oil to the fennel and make a cheese-topped version of this dish. Add 60ml/4 tbsp finely grated strong-flavoured cheese, such as mature Cheddar, Red Leicester or Parmesan, to the breadcrumb mixture in step 2. For an authentic Italian flavour, try using Fontina or Caciota cheese.

potato & mustard gratin

FINELY CUT POTATOES, INTERSPERSED WITH **GARLIC** AND **MUSTARD BUTTER** AND BAKED UNTIL **CRISP** AND **GOLDEN**, ARE **PERFECT** TO SERVE WITH A **GREEN SALAD**, OR AS A **SIDE DISH** ACCOMPANIMENT TO A **VEGETABLE** OR **NUT ROAST**.

ingredients

4 large **potatoes**, total weight about 900g/2lb

25g/1oz/2 tbsp **butter**

15ml/1 tbsp **olive oil**

2 large **garlic cloves**, crushed

30ml/2 tbsp **Dijon mustard**

15ml/1 tbsp **lemon juice**

15ml/1 tbsp fresh **thyme leaves**, plus extra to garnish

50ml/2fl oz/¼ cup **vegetable**

stock or **bouillon**

salt and freshly ground **black pepper**

method

SERVES 4

1 Slice the potatoes very thinly using a knife or the slicing attachment on a food processor. Place in a bowl of cold water to prevent them from discolouring.

2 Preheat the oven to 200°C/400°F/Gas 6. Heat the butter and oil in a flameproof casserole. Add the garlic and fry over a moderate heat for 3 minutes until light golden, stirring to prevent the garlic burning.

3 Stir in the Dijon mustard, lemon juice and half the thyme. Remove from the heat and pour the mixture into a jug.

4 Drain the potatoes and pat dry with kitchen paper. Place a layer of potatoes in the casserole, season to taste with salt and pepper and pour over one-third of the butter mixture. Place another layer of potatoes on top, season again, and pour over half the remaining butter mixture. Arrange a final layer of potatoes on top, pour over the remaining butter mixture and then add the stock. Season and sprinkle with the reserved thyme.

5 Cover the top with greaseproof paper and bake for 1 hour, then remove and discard the greaseproof paper and cook for a further 15 minutes, or until golden. Serve immediately.

garlic mashed sweet potato

DELICIOUS MASHED WITH **GARLICKY** BUTTER, ORANGE-FLESHED **SWEET POTATOES** NOT ONLY **LOOK GOOD**, THEY'RE **PACKED** WITH **VITAMINS**.

ingredients

4 large **sweet potatoes**, total weight about 900g/2lb, cubed

40g/1½oz/3 tbsp **unsalted butter**

3 **garlic cloves**, crushed

salt and freshly ground **black pepper**

method

SERVES 4

1 Cook the sweet potatoes in a large saucepan of boiling lightly salted water for about 15 minutes, or until tender. Drain thoroughly and return to the pan.

2 Melt the butter in a heavy-based saucepan. Add the garlic and sauté over a low heat for 1–2 minutes, until light golden, stirring to prevent the garlic from burning.

3 Pour the garlic butter over the sweet potatoes, season to taste with salt and pepper, and mash thoroughly until smooth and creamy. Transfer to a warm serving dish and serve immediately

cook's tip

If the sweet potatoes seem to be a little dry when you are mashing them, you can add 15–30ml/1–2 tbsp milk. For extra flavour, add some chopped fresh herbs, such as parsley, coriander or marjoram.

mushroom pilau

THIS DISH IS **SIMPLICITY ITSELF**. SERVE WITH ANY **INDIAN DISH**, SUCH AS A **VEGETABLE CURRY** OR **BIRYANI**. IT ALSO GOES WELL WITH **GRILLS** AND **BAKES**.

method

SERVES 4

1 Heat the oil in a flameproof casserole. Add the shallots, garlic and cardamom pods and fry over a medium heat, stirring occasionally, for 3–4 minutes, until the shallots have softened and are just beginning to turn golden brown.

2 Add the ghee or butter to the casserole. When it has melted, add the mushrooms and fry gently for 2–3 minutes.

3 Add the rice, ginger and garam masala. Stir-fry over a low heat for 2–3 minutes, then stir in the water and a little salt. Bring to the boil, then cover tightly and simmer over a very low heat for 10 minutes.

4 Remove the casserole from the heat. Leave to stand, covered, for 5 minutes. Add the chopped coriander and fork it through the rice. Spoon into a warm serving bowl and serve at once.

cook's tip
This pilau would be particularly delicious made with wild mushrooms, such as ceps, chanterelles, morels or field mushrooms. These tend to be rather expensive, however, so a good compromise would be a mixture of wild and cultivated mushrooms, such as button or chestnut.

ingredients

30ml/2 tbsp **vegetable oil**
2 **shallots**, finely chopped
1 **garlic** clove, crushed
3 **green cardamom** pods
25g/1oz/2 tbsp vegetable **ghee** or **butter**
175g/6oz/2¼ cups **button mushrooms**, sliced
225g/8oz/generous 1 cup **basmati rice**, soaked
5ml/1 tsp grated fresh **root ginger**
pinch of **garam masala**
450ml/¾ pint/scant 2 cups **water**
15ml/1 tbsp chopped fresh **coriander**
salt

AS WITH ALL **FRIED RICE DISHES**, THE **IMPORTANT** THING IS TO **MAKE SURE** THE COOKED RICE IS **COLD**. ADD IT **AFTER** COOKING ALL THE **OTHER INGREDIENTS**, AND STIR WELL TO HEAT IT THROUGH **COMPLETELY**.

californian citrus fried rice

method

SERVES 4–6

1 Beat the eggs with the vinegar and 10ml/2 tsp of the soy sauce. Heat 15ml/1 tbsp of the oil in a wok and cook the eggs until lightly scrambled. Transfer to a plate and set aside.

2 Add the cashew nuts to the wok and stir-fry for 1–2 minutes, until just golden. Transfer to a separate plate.

3 Heat the remaining oil in the wok. Add the garlic and spring onions and cook over a medium heat, stirring frequently, for 1–2 minutes, until the spring onions are beginning to soften, then add the carrots and stir-fry for 4 minutes.

4 Add the asparagus and cook for 2–3 minutes, then stir in the mushrooms and stir-fry for 1 further minute. Stir in the rice wine, the remaining soy sauce and the water. Simmer for a few minutes until the vegetables are just tender but still firm.

5 Add all the ingredients for the dressing to the wok, mix well and bring to the boil, then add the rice, scrambled eggs and cashew nuts. Toss over a low heat for 3–4 minutes, until the rice is heated through.

6 Just before serving, stir in the sesame oil and the grapefruit or orange segments. Garnish with strips of orange rind and serve at once.

ingredients

4 **eggs**

10ml/2 tsp **Japanese rice vinegar**

30ml/2 tbsp **light soy sauce**

about 45ml/3 tbsp **groundnut oil**

50g/2oz/½ cup **cashew nuts**

2 **garlic** cloves, crushed

6 **spring onions**, sliced diagonally

2 small **carrots**, cut into julienne strips

225g/8oz **asparagus**, each spear cut diagonally into 4 pieces

175g/6oz **button mushrooms**, halved

30ml/2 tbsp **rice wine**

30ml/2 tbsp **water**

450g/1lb/2¾ cups cooked **long grain white rice**

10ml/2 tsp **sesame oil**

1 **pink grapefruit** or **orange**, segmented

strips of **orange rind**, to garnish

For the hot dressing

5ml/1 tsp grated **orange rind**

30ml/2 tbsp **Japanese rice wine**

45ml/3 tbsp **oyster sauce**

30ml/2 tbsp freshly squeezed **pink grapefruit** or **orange juice**

5ml/1 tsp **medium** or **hot chilli sauce**

breads

ingredients

225g/8oz/2 cups
wholemeal flour
115g/4oz/1 cup **strong**
plain flour
5ml/1 tsp **salt**
2.5ml/½ tsp **bicarbonate**
of soda
5ml/1 tsp **cream of tartar**
2.5ml/½ tsp **chilli powder**
50g/2oz/¼ cup **soft margarine**
60ml/4 tbsp chopped mixed
fresh **herbs**
250ml/8fl oz/1 cup
skimmed milk
15ml/1 tbsp **sesame seeds**

cook's tip
To make sun-dried tomato triangles,
replace the mixed fresh herbs with
30ml/2 tbsp drained and chopped
sun-dried tomatoes in oil, and add
15ml/1 tbsp each mild paprika,
chopped fresh parsley and chopped
fresh marjoram.

wholemeal herb triangles

STUFFED WITH **SALAD**, THESE LITTLE
TRIANGLES MAKE A GOOD **LUNCHTIME**
SNACK. THEY ARE ALSO AN IDEAL
ACCOMPANIMENT TO A **BOWL** OF
STEAMING SOUP.

method

MAKES 8

1 Preheat the oven to 220°C/425°F/Gas 7. Lightly flour a baking sheet.
Put the wholemeal flour in a mixing bowl and sift in the remaining dry
ingredients, including the chilli powder, then rub in the soft margarine.

2 Add the herbs and milk and mix quickly to a soft dough. Turn on
to a lightly floured surface. Knead only very briefly or the dough will
become tough. Roll out to a 23cm/9in round and place on the
prepared baking sheet. Brush lightly with water and sprinkle evenly
with sesame seeds.

3 Carefully cut the dough round into eight wedges, separate them
slightly and bake for 15–20 minutes. Transfer to a wire rack to cool.
Serve warm or cold.

cheese & onion herb sticks

AN **EXTREMELY TASTY** BREAD WHICH IS VERY **GOOD** WITH **SOUP** OR **SALADS**. USE AN **EXTRA-STRONG CHEESE** TO GIVE **PLENTY** OF **FLAVOUR**.

method

MAKES 2 STICKS, EACH SERVING 4–6

1 Put the water in a jug. Sprinkle the yeast on top. Add the sugar, mix well and set aside for 10 minutes.

2 Heat the oil in a frying pan. Add the onion and fry over a medium heat, stirring frequently, for 5–6 minutes, until the onion is soft and coloured golden brown.

3 Sift the flour, salt and mustard powder into a mixing bowl. Add the herbs. Set aside 30ml/2 tbsp of the cheese and stir the remainder into the flour mixture. Make a well in the centre. Add the yeast mixture, together with the fried onions and oil from the pan, then gradually incorporate the flour and mix to a soft dough, adding extra water if necessary.

4 Turn the dough on to a floured surface and knead for 5 minutes, until smooth and elastic. Return to the clean bowl, cover with a damp dish towel and leave in a warm place to rise for about 2 hours, until doubled in bulk. Lightly grease two baking sheets.

5 Turn the dough on to a floured surface, knead briefly, then divide the mixture in half and roll each piece into a 30cm/12in long stick. Place each stick on a baking sheet and make diagonal cuts along the top.

6 Sprinkle the sticks with the reserved cheese. Cover and set aside for 30 minutes, until well risen. Preheat the oven to 220°C/425°F/Gas 7. Bake the sticks for 25 minutes, or until they sound hollow when they are tapped underneath. Cool on a wire rack.

ingredients

300ml/½ pint/1¼ cups
warm **water**
5ml/1 tsp **dried yeast**
pinch of **sugar**
15ml/1 tbsp **sunflower oil**
1 **red onion**, chopped
450g/1 lb/4 cups **strong white flour**
5ml/1 tsp **salt**
5ml/1 tsp **dry mustard powder**
45ml/3 tbsp chopped fresh **herbs,** such as **thyme, marjoram, sage**
75g/3oz/¾ cup grated **Cheddar cheese**

cook's tip
To make onion and coriander sticks, omit the cheese, herbs and mustard. Add 15ml/1 tbsp ground coriander and 45ml/3 tbsp chopped fresh coriander instead.

spicy millet bread

THIS IS A FABULOUS **SPICY BREAD** WITH A **GOLDEN CRUST**. CUT THE BREAD INTO **WEDGES**, AS YOU WOULD A CAKE, AND **SERVE WARM** WITH A THICK **VEGETABLE SOUP**.

ingredients

200ml/7fl oz/scant 1 cup **water**
90g/3½oz/½ cup **millet**
550g/1lb 6oz/5½ cups **strong unbleached plain flour**
10ml/2 tsp **salt**
5ml/1 tsp **sugar**
5ml/1 tsp **dried chilli flakes** (optional)
7g/¼oz sachet **easy-blend dried yeast**
350ml/12fl oz/1½ cups warm **water**
25g/1oz/2 tbsp **unsalted butter**
1 **onion**, roughly chopped
15ml/1 tbsp **cumin seeds**
5ml/1 tsp **ground turmeric**

cook's tip

Strong flour is usually used for yeast cookery, especially when making breads. It is milled from durum wheat, rather than the soft wheat used for plain and self-raising flour. It has a higher protein content and more gluten, resulting in a smooth, elastic dough.

method

MAKES 1 LOAF

1 Bring the cold water to the boil, add the millet, cover and simmer over a low heat for 20 minutes, until the grains are soft and the water is absorbed. Remove the pan from the heat and set aside to cool until just warm.

2 Mix together the flour, salt, sugar, chilli flakes, if using, and yeast in a large bowl. Stir in the millet, then add the warm water and mix to form a soft dough.

3 Turn out the dough on to a floured work surface and knead for 10 minutes, until it is smooth and elastic.

4 Place the dough in an oiled bowl and cover with oiled clear film or a dish towel. Set aside to rise in a warm place for 1 hour, until doubled in bulk.

5 Meanwhile, melt the butter in a heavy-based frying pan. Add the onion and fry over a low heat, stirring occasionally, for 10 minutes, until softened and golden. Add the cumin seeds and turmeric and fry, stirring constantly, for a further 5–8 minutes, until the cumin seeds begin to pop. Remove the pan from the heat and set aside.

6 Knock back the dough by pressing down with your knuckles to deflate it, then shape into a round. Place the onion mixture in the middle of the dough and bring the sides over the filling to enclose it and make a parcel, then seal well.

7 Place the loaf on an oiled baking sheet, seam side down, cover with oiled clear film and set aside in a warm place for 45 minutes, until doubled in bulk. Preheat the oven to 220°C/425°F/Gas 7.

8 Bake the bread for 30 minutes, until golden. It should sound hollow when tapped underneath. Leave to cool on a wire rack.

sweet potato & honey rolls

THESE **SWEET** ROLLS **TASTE** JUST AS **GOOD** **SERVED** WITH **FRUIT CONSERVES** AS WITH **CHEESE** OR A **SAVOURY SOUP**.

method

MAKES 12

1 Cook the sweet potato in plenty of boiling water for 45 minutes, or until very tender. Preheat the oven to 220°C/425°F/Gas 7.

2 Meanwhile, sift the flour into a large bowl, add the yeast, ground nutmeg and cumin seeds. Stir thoroughly.

3 Mix the honey and milk together. Drain the potato and peel the skin. Mash the potato flesh and add to the flour, together with the honey and milk mixture.

4 Bring the mixture together and knead for 5 minutes on a floured surface. Place the dough in a bowl and cover with a damp dish towel. Set aside to rise for 30 minutes.

5 Turn the dough out and knock back to remove any air bubbles. Divide the dough into 12 pieces and shape each one into a round.

6 Place the rolls on a greased baking sheet. Cover with a damp dish towel and set to rise in a warm place for 30 minutes, or until doubled in size.

7 Bake for 10 minutes. Remove from the oven and drizzle with more honey and scatter over more cumin seeds before serving.

ingredients

1 large **sweet potato**

225g/8oz/2 cups **strong white flour**

5ml/1 tsp **easy-blend dried yeast**

pinch of **ground nutmeg**

pinch of **cumin seeds**, plus extra for scattering

5ml/1 tsp **clear honey**, plus extra for drizzling

200ml/7fl oz/scant 1 cup warm **milk**

oil, for greasing

cook's tip
Honey may be blended or single-flower. The former tends to have quite a bland flavour, while the latter varies depending on the type of flowers it is made from. Popular single-flower honeys include acacia, clover, heather, Hymettus, orange blossom, rosemary and thyme.

THE BASIC **ARAB BREADS** OF THE **LEVANT** AND **GULF REGIONS** HAVE **TRADITIONALLY** BEEN MADE WITH A FINELY GROUND **WHOLEMEAL FLOUR** SIMILAR TO **CHAPATI FLOUR**, BUT ARE NOW BEING MADE WITH **WHITE FLOUR** AS WELL.

ingredients

450g/1lb/4 cups **unbleached strong white flour**
5ml/1 tsp **salt**
20g/¾ oz **fresh yeast**
280ml/9fl oz/scant 1¼ cups warm **water**

For the topping
60ml/4 tbsp finely chopped **onion**
5ml/1 tsp **ground cumin**
10ml/2 tsp **ground coriander**
10ml/2 tsp chopped fresh **mint**
30ml/2 tbsp **olive oil**

onion bread

method

MAKES 8

1 Lightly flour two baking sheets. Sift the flour and salt together into a large bowl and make a well in the centre. Cream the yeast with a little of the water, then mix in the remainder

2 Add the yeast mixture to the well in the centre of the flour and mix to a firm dough. Turn out on to a lightly floured surface and knead for 8–10 minutes, until smooth and elastic.

3 Place in a clean bowl, cover with lightly oiled clear film and set aside to rise in a warm place for 1 hour, until the dough has doubled in bulk.

4 Knock back the dough and turn out on to a lightly floured surface. Divide into eight equal pieces and roll into 13–15cm/5–6in rounds. Make them slightly concave. Prick all over with a fork and space well apart on the baking sheets. Cover with lightly oiled clear film and set aside to rise for 15–20 minutes.

5 Meanwhile, preheat the oven to 200°C/400°F/Gas 6. Mix the chopped onion, ground cumin, ground coriander and chopped mint in a bowl. Brush the breads with the olive oil for the topping, sprinkle them evenly with the spicy onion mixture and bake for 15–20 minutes. Serve the onion breads warm.

cook's tip
Try different varieties of mint, such as apple, pineapple or lemon mint, which have flavoured undertones. If fresh mint is not available, then add 15ml/1 tbsp dried mint. Use the freeze-dried variety, if you can, as it has much more flavour.

olive & herb bread

OLIVE BREADS ARE **POPULAR** ALL OVER THE **MEDITERRANEAN**. FOR THIS **GREEK RECIPE** USE RICH, **OILY OLIVES**, OR THOSE **MARINATED** IN **HERBS**, RATHER THAN CANNED ONES.

ingredients

30ml/2 tbsp **olive oil**

2 **red onions**, thinly sliced

750g/1⅔lb/7 cups **strong white flour**

7.5ml/1½ tsp **salt**

20ml/4 tsp **easy-blend dried yeast**

45ml/3 tbsp roughly chopped fresh **parsley**

45ml/3 tbsp roughly chopped fresh **coriander** or **mint**

225g/8oz/1⅓ cups pitted **black** or **green olives**

475ml/16fl oz/2 cups warm **water**

cook's tip
If you prefer, shape the dough into 16 small rolls. Slash the tops as described in step 5 and reduce the cooking time to 25 minutes.

method

MAKES 2 x 675G/1½LB LOAVES

1 Heat the oil in a heavy-based frying pan. Add the onions and fry over a medium heat, stirring occasionally, for 5–8 minutes, until soft and golden brown.

2 Sift the flour and salt into a large mixing bowl. Add the yeast, parsley, coriander or mint, olives and fried onions and pour in the warm water.

3 Mix to a dough, using a round-bladed knife, adding a little more warm water if the mixture feels dry.

4 Turn out on to a lightly floured surface and knead well for about 10 minutes, until the dough is elastic. Put it into a clean bowl, cover with lightly oiled clear film and set aside to rise in a warm place until doubled in bulk.

5 Preheat the oven to 220°C/425°F/Gas 7. Lightly grease two baking sheets. Turn the dough on to a floured surface and cut in half. Shape into two rounds and place on the baking sheets. Cover loosely with lightly oiled clear film and set aside until doubled in size.

6 Slash the tops of the loaves with a knife, then bake for about 40 minutes, or until the loaves sound hollow when tapped on the bottom. Transfer to a wire rack to cool.

THIS IS A **FLATTISH BREAD**, ORIGINATING FROM **GENOA** IN ITALY, MADE WITH **FLOUR**, **OLIVE OIL** AND **SALT**. THERE ARE **VARIATIONS**, FROM MANY **REGIONS** OF ITALY, INCLUDING **STUFFED VARIETIES**, AND VERSIONS **TOPPED** WITH **ONIONS**, **OLIVES** OR **HERBS**.

ingredients

25g/1oz **fresh yeast**
120ml/4fl oz/½ cup warm **water**
400g/14oz/3½ cups **strong white flour**
10ml/2 tsp **salt**
75ml/5 tbsp **olive oil**
10ml/2 tsp **coarse sea salt**

focaccia

method

MAKES 1 ROUND 25CM/10IN LOAF

1 Dissolve the yeast in the warm water in a small bowl and set aside for 10 minutes.

2 Sift the flour and salt into a large bowl, make a well in the centre, and add the yeast mixture and 30ml/2 tbsp of the olive oil. Mix in the flour and add more water, if necessary, to make a dough.

3 Turn out on to a floured work surface and knead the dough thoroughly for about 10 minutes, until smooth and elastic. Return to the clean bowl, cover with a dish towel, and set aside to rise in a warm place for about 2–2½ hours, until the dough has doubled in bulk.

4 Knock back the dough and knead again for a few minutes. Press into an oiled 25cm/10in tart tin, and cover with a damp dish towel. Set aside to rise for 30 minutes.

5 Preheat the oven to 200°C/400°F/Gas 6. Poke the dough all over with your fingers to make little dimples in the surface. Pour the remaining oil over the dough, using a pastry brush to take it to the edges. Sprinkle with the sea salt.

6 Bake for 20–25 minutes, until the bread is a pale gold. Carefully remove from the tin and leave to cool on a rack. The bread is best eaten on the same day, but it also freezes very well.

sun-dried tomato bread

IN **SOUTHERN ITALY**, **TOMATOES** ARE OFTEN **DRIED** OFF IN THE **HOT SUN**. THEY ARE THEN **PRESERVED** IN **OIL** OR **HUNG UP** IN THE **KITCHEN** TO USE IN THE **WINTER**. THIS RECIPE USES **THE FORMER** TECHNIQUE.

method

MAKES 4 SMALL LOAVES

1 Sift the flour, salt and sugar into a bowl and make a well in the centre. Crumble the yeast, mix with 150ml/¼ pint/⅔ cup of the warm milk and add to the flour.

2 Mix the tomato purée into the remaining milk, until evenly blended, then add to the flour, together with the oil from the jar of sun-dried tomatoes and olive oil.

3 Gradually mix the flour into the liquid ingredients to make a dough. Turn on to a floured surface, and knead for about 10 minutes, until smooth and elastic. Return to the clean bowl, cover with a damp dish towel and set aside to rise in a warm place for about 2 hours.

4 Knock back the dough and add the tomatoes and onion. Knead until evenly distributed through the dough. Shape into four rounds and place on a greased baking sheet. Cover with a damp dish towel and set aside to rise for about 45 minutes.

5 Preheat the oven to 190°C/375°F/Gas 5. Bake the bread for 45 minutes, or until the loaves sound hollow when tapped underneath. Leave to cool on a wire rack. Serve warm or lightly toasted and topped with grated mozzarella cheese.

ingredients

675g/1½lb/6 cups **strong white flour**
10ml/2 tsp **salt**
25g/1oz/2 tbsp **caster sugar**
25g/1oz **fresh yeast**
400–475ml/14–16fl oz/ 1⅔–2 cups warm **milk**
15ml/1 tbsp **tomato purée**
75ml/5 tbsp **oil** from the jar of **sun-dried tomatoes**
75ml/5 tbsp **extra virgin olive oil**
75g/3oz/¾ cup drained **sun-dried tomatoes**, chopped
1 large **onion**, chopped
mozzarella cheese, to serve

cook's tip
The quickest and easiest way to chop sun-dried tomatoes is to cut them up with a pair of sharp kitchen scissors.

index